SECURE

SECURE

LEANING ON GOD IN ECONOMIC TURMOIL

David Wilkerson

World Challenge

Secure
Copyright © 2020 by World Challenge

Requests for information should be addressed to World Challenge, 1125 Kelly Johnson Blvd Suite 321, Colorado Springs, CO 80920

ISBN 978-0-578-76917-2

Library of Congress Cataloging-in-Publication Data
Names: Wilkerson, David, author
Title: Secure: leaning on God in economic turmoil / David Wilkerson.
Description: Colorado Springs, Colorado : World Challenge, [2020]
Identifiers: ISBN 9780578769172 (paperback)
Subjects: LCSH: Religious aspects--Christianity.
Classification: [Copyright office issue]

Original Copyright 1998 / ISBN 09663172-2-X

Scripture quotations marked KJV are taken from the King James Version. Public domain.

Cover design by Alexia DeLong

First edition 1998 / Second edition 2020 / Printed in the United States of America

TABLE OF CONTENTS

Foreword   5

Introduction   7

Chapter 1 : Lessons from the Great Depression   9

Chapter 2 : Biblical Prosperity in Hardship   24

Chapter 3 : Preparing for Hard Times   39

Chapter 4 : The Preservation of Zion   53

Chapter 5 : God's Controversy Concerning Zion   66

Chapter 6 : Protection in the Coming Storm   82

Chapter 7 : Armageddon and the Mark of the Beast   92

Chapter 8 : Craving the Presence of the Lord   105

Chapter 9 : Not Fully Trusting God   119

Chapter 10 : The Secret to Strength   132

Chapter 11 : Awakened Through Suffering   146

Chapter 12 : Finding Rest Amid Difficulties   160

Chapter 13 : Final Thoughts   175

Scriptures to Live by in Perilous Times   178

FOREWORD

The year was 1999, and public anxieties were growing as people looked forward to the new millennium. Speculation ran wild that these new computer systems, which businesses and government organizations had quickly come to rely on, would malfunction when they had to process the number 2000.

As the end of the year drew closer, people began hoarding food and buying books on survival skills while others purchased extra insurance policies and speculated that this future event could lead to a serious economic downturn for the United States and much of the developed world. A kind of hysteria gripped many people at the idea that the world, as they had known it, could change so swiftly.

David Wilkerson was leading Times Square Church at the time and was receiving anxious letters and questions from believers not only in his own church but from around the country.

Not one to brush off people's honest and heart-felt concerns, he went into a time of serious contemplation and prayer. The book *God's Plan to Protect His People in the Coming Depression* was the result of his earnest soul-searching and prayer.

We believe that the truths he expressed are eternal

and have refined the message for this rerelease of that original edition. We sought to preserve David's deep convictions about how God's children must respond to hardship and economic difficulties. He acknowledges the responsibilities that we have to be good stewards of our resources, particularly those of a financial nature, but he also speaks out against the panic and worry that seemed to have gripped the population. More than anything, he urges believers to seek a closer relationship with our Father who graciously provides for his children and who gives us the Spirit of peace.

While the year 2000's predicted disaster never materialized, the wisdom and biblical nature of David Wilkerson's advice remains very much apropos.

The Bible promises that we will face trials and tribulation in this life, and David wished to see God-fearing people prepared spiritually and financially for this future. Out of respect for his wishes and life-long mission, we have edited and re-released this book so that it may be a blessing to the church today.

INTRODUCTION

Ominous storm clouds have gathered above our nation, and they're mounting higher and higher. A *Newsweek* cover screams, "Global Crash." The *New York Times* announces, "Wall Street Gloom Shakes Confidence. Markets Quake." Voices of reason keep crying out from every corner, trying to warn us of coming financial calamities.

Yet these warnings are being wholly ignored by those who should be alarmed. As a result, we're witnessing a tragic repeat of the mistakes and apathy that preceded the Great Depression of the 1930s. Years ago, President Calvin Coolidge turned a deaf ear to the many warnings of an impending financial crash. Then later, in the midst of the depression, President Herbert Hoover ignored the warnings of the opposition party, who said America was falling into an ever-deepening crisis. President Hoover responded, "It's almost over. The fundamentals of our nation are all sound. There is nothing to worry about."

It's time we faced the truth. America is on a fast track to a full-blown depression that could end up much worse than the Great Depression of the 1930s.

Let me reassure you, however. This book is not about the bad news facing our nation. Rather, it is about the good and comforting news of God's covenant promises to preserve and protect his people through every storm.

In 1998 before the Y2K scare, our offices were inundated with appeals for financial advice and words of encouragement. The requests came from Christians who were overwhelmed with fears about the future. Their most-asked question was, "How can we prepare for what's coming? We agree, there is a storm on the horizon. But isn't there a word of encouragement for us from the Lord, something to help us through it all?"

I sought God diligently for a message of hope, comfort and direction. I reasoned with him, "Lord, if you put on my heart warnings about a coming depression, then you also have to give me a message of hope."

I believe he has.

If you expect to find detailed advice for your stock investments in this book, you'll be disappointed. I'm neither an economist nor a financial advisor. If you're a lover of Jesus and a respecter of the holy scriptures, though, I believe you'll discover in these pages God's plan to keep his people in the coming depression. May faith arise in your heart and evict all fear as you read this message of hope.

When you see judgments come to pass, go straight to God's word. Then pick up this book and encourage yourself in the Lord. If not today, then someday you're going to need the spiritual encouragement this hopeful message offers.

If you are a true believer, you are the apple of God's eye, his beloved bride. He has given you an ironclad promise to keep you to the very end!

Chapter One

Lessons from the Great Depression

"The industrial situation of the United States is absolutely sound, and our credit situation is in no way critical... The interest given by all the public to brokers' loans is always exaggerated... The markets generally are now in a healthy condition. The last six weeks have done an immense amount of good by shaking down prices... I know of nothing wrong with the stock market or with the underlying business and credit structure."

– Charles Mitchell, Chairman of National City Bank of New York, two days before the stock market crash on October 22, 1929

The time was the Roaring Twenties, and Americans were enjoying the greatest prosperity in the nation's history. Very few people saw the storm clouds gathering overhead. Most people's thoughts and energies were focused on making money. This period was also known as the "decade of decadence" During this time, God gave the world a lesson about his wrath against nations that sin against his mercy. He sent a warning to America in the form of a major depression, and this terrible judgment immediately brought the Roaring Twenties to a sudden halt.

In a single ten-year period, from 1919 to 1929, America changed from a society of mostly religious, well-mannered citizens to a nation saturated with drunkenness, licentiousness and obsession with sex. Two main factors contributed to this change: the inventions of the radio and the closed-top automobile. Up to that time, most cars had no tops. But with the advent of the enclosed car came a sexual revolution. Unmarried couples started using their newfound privacy for sex. This moral upheaval prompted the newspapers of the time to label the new cars "brothels on wheels."

In 1920, the women's suffrage movement gave American women the right to vote, an event said to have liberated the modern woman. Yet this landmark act also ushered in other forms of "liberation" regarding women. Up to this time, women were said to be the guardians of morality in America. But suddenly, as women gained more freedom, the hems of their skirts began to rise higher and higher. Until 1919, women wore dresses that were so long, they virtually scraped the ground. Now, as the new immorality of the twenties took root, dress codes changed drastically. The new decade became the era of flappers, young women who wore thin, form-fitting dresses in an effort to shake off the old Victorian moral codes.

This change in dress was so unprecedented and so abrupt, an alarmed fashion writer for the New York Times declared, "The American woman has lifted skirts far beyond any modest limitation." Another writer warned, "If (dresses' hems) are nine inches off the ground today, there could come a day when our nation becomes so immoral, hems will rise to the kneecaps." These weren't the rantings of conservative preachers but of the unconverted press! What would they think of today's mini-skirts, revealing dresses and near-nude bathing suits?

In retrospect, it's easy to be amused by the eroding morals of the twenties. Preachers of the time denounced women who wore rouge, calling them "painted ladies." They even cried out against women who bobbed their hair or rode bicycles on Sundays. But in truth, the acceleration of bad manners and morals in the twenties was no laughing matter. Suddenly, the upright morality of the past was being mocked, and the result was disastrous.

Smoking became pandemic. So-called "nice girls" began to light up cigarettes in public, just like men. And while their male counterparts carried hip-flasks full of whiskey, women even began chewing tobacco and spitting in spittoons.

Soon, an obsession with sex swept the nation like wildfire. The subject became a daily focus of conversation. Sex-centered Freudian philosophy swept the land, and religious convictions about sex were ridiculed. Public dancing became sensual and intimate, and sex in movies and magazines grew permissive by the period's standards. (There was even some nudity in films and publications of the time, before the censor codes were put into place.)

At this point, liberal preachers who prided themselves on keeping up with the times dismissed all warnings of a moral landslide. They tried to reassure an alarmed public that the sexual experimentation of the period wouldn't escalate into deeper immorality. They even made light of young people smoking, drinking gin, dancing sensually and having sex in the back seats of cars.

But the situation was rapidly getting worse. By 1923 young women were crowding into bars during cocktail hour, just like men, hiking their feet up on the bar rail, getting drunk and having to be carried out to their cars. Along with strong drink came even stronger words. Language suddenly turned foul and indecent. God's name was cursed everywhere, an act unthinkable just a few years before.

Not surprisingly, the standards and codes of marriage began to break down. Chastity and faithfulness grew outdated, and adultery became vogue. Over time, the new sexual immorality broke up homes all across the country. In 1910, almost nine marriages out of one hundred ended in divorce. By 1920, that percentage had risen to more than thirteen, and by 1928 it ballooned to one in six marriages.

Such drastic changes are hard to fathom, even by today's standards. Yet they all happened in just a few short years.

By 1928, America was a wild, roaring, prosperous nation. Just like today, America in the Roaring Twenties enjoyed a seven-year bull market, from 1923 to 1929. The country's prosperity seemed endless. Stocks in railroad companies skyrocketed, even as the automobile industry produced tens of millions of cars. Radio was booming, and the value of companies such as General Electric, Woolworth and Montgomery Ward escalated out of sight.

When Herbert Hoover was elected president in 1928, the country was still riding high on the prosperity that had begun under Calvin Coolidge. President Hoover declared in his acceptance speech, "We in America today are nearer to the final triumph over poverty than ever before in the history of the land. The poorhouse is vanishing. We are in sight of the day when poverty will be banished from this nation."

Money and sports became the two golden idols of the

time. Millions of people invested in the stock market, trying to strike it rich, and the market kept smashing all previous records. Everyone, it seemed, was playing the market – shoeshine men, bus drivers, housewives, maids, butlers, even ministers. One newspaper reported that four out of every five people who rode trolley cars were reading stock reports. Virtually every small city in the country had a brokerage house.

America's prosperity was so rampant, all rules of logic were broken. People reasoned, "Every crash in the past has been followed by a recovery. The market can only go up. Therefore, there's no reason to sell. I'll just buy and hold on."

In 1929, however, the Standard Trade and Securities Service began to sense that the market was headed for trouble. At one point they issued a stern warning. A handful of business leaders also awakened to the crisis, and they tried to sound an alarm about a possible crash. Several ministers joined in, denouncing America's widespread greed and prophesying that God was about to judge the country for its sins.

The vast majority of experts responded, "Be bullish on America! Prosperity is here to stay. Just keep investing and spending." One writer of the time summed up America's vision of the future with these words: "We are a country free from poverty and hardship. We have new science, new prosperity, roads crowded with millions of new automobiles. Airplanes are filling the skies. Lines of high-tension wires flow hilltop to hilltop with power to give information to a thousand labor-saving machines. Skyscrapers rise above one-time villages. Vast cities are rising up in great masses of stone and concrete and are roaring with incredibly mechanized traffic. And smartly dressed men and women are spending, spending, spending the money they have won in the market."

Americans ignored the few voices of reason who advised caution and just kept spending. Then the inevitable happened.

On September 3, 1929, the market began to crack. Something was wrong, and everybody in America knew it. Margin buyers suddenly began fleeing the market. Yet, even after this omen, economic soothsayers raised a loud voice to try to calm the panic. The Harvard Economic Society announced, "This is just a period of readjustment, a much-needed market correction. This is not the beginning of a depression." An expert named Professor Fisher declared, "Within a few months the market will rebound and go higher."

President Hoover echoed the feelings of most financial observers. "America's industrial situation is absolutely sound. Our factories are humming. Business is healthy. The economy is in good condition. There is nothing fundamentally wrong with our underlying business and credit structure. It's a good time to buy stock." One newspaper published this headline on October 16, 1929: "American business is too big and diversified, and the country too rich, to be influenced by stock fluctuations."

Finally, on Tuesday, October 29, 1929, the American stock market crashed to the ground. Utter fear and panic struck by noon that day. The leading stocks just kept falling, and this time there were no bargain hunters, investment buyers or big operators looking to buy back their own stock. Instead, all across the country, people swarmed into their local brokers' offices, desperate to sell at any price. But there simply were no buyers.

The exchange system couldn't cope with the masses

trying to sell. And, within eight short hours, the party was over. President Hoover tried to reassure the nation. But his words had little effect. The communications systems of America were jammed by the voices of sellers only, with no buyers in sight.

Panic hit the foreign nations. All across the world, people were stunned, shocked and fearful at the news that the great economy of America had suddenly fallen. In every town and village in the United States, families were cast into poverty, having lost their paper wealth. Soon suicides were being reported in areas all over the nation. The Great Depression had begun.

Consider what one writer said of the crash's aftermath: "There was hardly a man or woman in the country whose attitude toward life had not been affected by it to some degree...hope was suddenly shattered. With the market in shambles and prosperity folding, Americans were soon to find themselves living in a different world, everything changed. Day by day, the newspapers printed the grim reports of suicides."

The deep depression lasted for nearly a decade.

What brought down the stock market in 1929? What was it, exactly, that shook America and the world during that time, turning prosperity into poverty overnight? What brought on that worldwide depression? Simply put, it was the Lord. It was the same God who destroyed Sodom and Gomorrah for their sins...the same God who judged Israel for its idolatry, bringing Titus' army down on Jerusalem to destroy it...the same God who promises in Revelation to wipe out the prosperity of Babylon in a single hour...the same God who has been warning America about its sin for years, through the voices of prophets who cry out with grieving, broken hearts.

Yes, America is a modern Babylon, and God's message to Babylon is this: "Thou saidst, I shall be a lady for ever: so that thou didst not lay these things to thy heart, neither didst remember the latter end of it. Therefore hear now this, thou that art given to pleasures, that dwellest carelessly, that sayest in thine heart, I am, and none else beside me; I shall not sit as a widow, neither shall I know the loss of children:

"But these two things shall come to thee in a moment in one day, the loss of children, and widowhood: they shall come upon thee in their perfection for the multitude of thy sorceries, and for the great abundance of thine enchantments. For thou hast trusted in thy wickedness: thou hast said, None seeth me. Thy wisdom and thy knowledge, it hath perverted thee; and thou hast said in thine heart, I am, and none else beside me.

"Therefore evil shall come upon thee; thou shalt not know from whence it riseth: and mischief shall fall upon thee; thou shalt not be able to put it off: and desolation shall come upon thee suddenly, which thou shalt not know" (Isaiah 47:7-11).

We have conveniently chosen to ignore the lessons of God's judgment on Egypt, Israel, Jerusalem, Sodom, Babylon and all other failed empires. Now, after just over half a century, we have totally forgotten the lessons God tried to teach us in the Great Depression of the thirties, a judgment that crippled our nation and the whole world.

God was saying to us then, "Flagrant sin is a reproach to any nation. So you must never forget how your country provoked me to wrath a generation ago. I had given you power to obtain wealth and become prosperous, so you could be a great missionary nation. But you quickly forgot me, the source of all your blessings. Therefore, I laid your nation low, humbling your proud markets and causing the rich to become poor. Remember that day, America. Consider what I did to the past generation, and don't make the same mistakes!"

Has this nation learned anything from its past? Have our government leaders considered God's historical judgments on wicked nations? No. They have ignored them all.

It's very clear the nations of the world today are making the same mistakes that brought down God's wrath upon every sinful society in the past. By all indications, every nation – including America – is continuing its path of godlessness, oblivious to God's warnings and judgments on all sides. Our leaders seem completely ignorant of the lessons of history, having no regard for the Lord's past dealings with sinful humankind. Instead, they're behaving like madmen, as if there isn't a God in heaven who will bring them to account.

By contrast, Moses commanded Israel to remember all of God's past dealings with their nation.

• "Thou...shalt well remember what the Lord thy God did unto Pharaoh, and unto all Egypt" (Deuteronomy 7:18).

• "Remember, and forget not, how thou provokedst the Lord thy God to wrath in the wilderness...so that the Lord was angry with you to have destroyed you" (Deuteronomy 9:7-8).

• "Thou shalt remember the Lord thy God: for it is he that giveth thee power to get wealth..." (Deuteronomy 8:18).

• "Beware that thou forget not the Lord thy God... who led thee through that great and terrible wilderness, wherein were fiery serpents, and scorpions, and drought, where there was no water; who brought thee forth water out of the rock of flint; who fed thee in the wilderness with manna, which thy fathers knew not, that he might humble thee, and that he might prove thee, to do thee good at thy latter end" (Deuteronomy 8:11, 15-16).

God was warning his people: "Look back, and remember well how I dealt with your sinful ancestors. I judged them in my wrath, reducing them to poverty, sending depression and deprivation upon them. Remember, too, how I provided miracles and supernatural deliverances to your fathers when they turned back to me. I want you to remember both of these things about me, because I never change. I am the same yesterday, today and forever, and I will act in the same way toward you in your situation right now. I'll send both judgment on the wicked and provision for the repentant. So, my children, learn from your past, and don't make the same mistakes your fathers did."

Moses then instructed the people, "Remember the days of old, consider the years of many generations: ask thy father, and he will shew thee; thy elders, and they will tell thee" (Deuteronomy 32:7). He was telling them, "Learn from your fathers and elders, those who have gone before you. Go back and examine the record of their history. See how I brought judgment upon them, and learn from their mistakes. You need to be familiar with my dealings with all the nations because I'm going to deal with you in the same way."

King Josiah heeded lessons from the past. When Josiah took the throne in Israel, his high priest reported that a book had been found recording all of God's past dealings with Israel. The book was then brought to Josiah and read to him. At that point, scripture says, "...when the king had heard the words of the book of the law, that he rent his clothes" (2 Kings 22:11).

Suddenly, Josiah's eyes were opened by the hearing of God's word. He was so shocked by how far Israel had strayed from the Lord, he tore his outer garment. He cried out to his confidants, "If this is all true, if this is how God has judged former generations for their sins, then we're in real danger. God's wrath is already kindled against us!"

Josiah then instructed the priest, "Go ye, enquire of the Lord for me, and for the people, and for all Judah, concerning the words of this book that is found: for great is the wrath of the Lord that is kindled against us, because our fathers have not hearkened unto the words of this book, to do according unto all that which is written concerning us" (2 Kings 22:13).

King Josiah did just as Moses had commanded: He studied history and recalled God's dealings with former generations. He learned what kind of behavior brought down God's wrath upon them. He examined the present condition of his own nation. After all of this, Josiah concluded, "We've sinned worse than our fathers did before us. And if the Lord judged them at that time, he has to judge us today. Our society is on the brink of judgment even now."

Let me ask you, do you know of any government leader, either in America or in any other nation who has seen the coming global disaster and has stopped to consider God's ways? Is any leader aware that God's wrath is kindled against this generation? Does any leader have the boldness to admit, "We've sinned worse than our ancestors did, even in the decade of decadence. We're far more wicked than they were, and God judged them with the Great Depression. If the Lord smote them for lesser sins, how can we expect to be spared? We're in serious danger!"

You don't have to be a prophet to know the history of God's dealings with sinful nations. It's all revealed very clearly in his word. Moreover, I believe every minister of the gospel is called to warn God's people about such judgments. Yet, where are the preachers today who will rise up as Josiah did, searching God's word and sounding the alarm, crying, "We've become a generation of insolent, arrogant, depraved people. We're a hundred times more wicked than our fathers were in the Roaring Twenties. We're in grave danger. It's time to repent and clothe ourselves in the sackcloth of godly sorrow."

As a minister of the gospel, I can't take lightly the awesome warning Ezekiel gives to all of God's watchmen. "If the watchman see the sword come, and blow not the trumpet, and the people be not warned; if the sword come, and take any person from among them, he is taken away in his iniquity; but his blood will I require at the watchman's hand" (Ezekiel 33:6). God is warning all ministers, "Any preacher of my gospel who doesn't search my word and examine history is not doing as Moses commanded. When the time comes for such lazy shepherds to stand before me at the judgment, they'll do so with blood on their hands!"

How can any minister who studies God's word and spends time in prayer not see what is coming? If he doesn't see the storm ahead, he must be blinded by either sensuality or apathy. Such a man isn't worthy of his calling. Yet, if he does see what's coming, he has to sound a warning. If he refuses to warn God's people and instead allows them to drift in sin and apathy, their lost souls will be charged to his account at the judgment.

May God help us to learn this lesson.

There is another lesson we have not learned from the past.The church of Jesus Christ in America today has not learned to trust the Lord fully in perilous times. We may have endured lesser tests in our lives – illnesses, griefs, losses, financial problems – but we have not learned the awful consequences of unbelief in dark, difficult days.

David said, "Our fathers trusted in thee: they trusted, and thou didst deliver them. They cried unto thee, and were delivered: they trusted in thee, and were not confounded" (Psalm 22:4-5). David himself was one of these faithful fathers. Indeed, he remains an example to us today of someone who fully trusted God. He testifies that he endured an awful period of pain in his life, in which he almost "fainted." But then he regained his faith and was able to say, "I...believed to see the goodness of the Lord in the land of the living" (Psalm 27:13). Psalm 91 is David's declaration of his trust in the Lord at all times, no matter what he faced in life.

Very few Christians today fully understand the incredible miracles and deliverances God performed for his people in the Old Testament. We've read about how God opened the Red Sea...how he provided water from a rock in the desert...how he caused manna to fall from heaven...how he delivered the Hebrew children from the fiery furnace and the lions' den...how he delivered Israel from Pharaoh, Goliath and many other enemies. Evidently, we haven't applied these lessons well enough to chase away our own panic when hard times arise. Now as we face the coming crisis, we're still not able to combat our flood of fears and anxieties sufficiently.

As we study the history of our forefathers, we discover

that many who enjoyed marvelous miracles in their life-times often fell into disbelief during later trials. In short, when they came to the hardest part of their testings, they failed God. The very fathers who once faithfully trusted God, and who experienced his delivering power time after time, voiced doubt and unbelief when they came up against new difficulties: "Behold, he smote the rock, that the waters gushed out, and the streams overflowed; can he give bread also? Can he provide flesh for his people?" (Psalm 78:20). Even after Israel experienced miracle after miracle of God's deliverance and provision, they still wondered, "Sure, God provided us with water. But can he give us food as well?"

When the Lord heard these murmurings from his people, he grew angry, "Because they believed not in God, and trusted not in his salvation" (Psalm 78:22). The psalmist is warning us in this verse: We can trust in God for years, seeing him perform miracle after miracle on our behalf, and yet we may face a calamity that suddenly sends us spiraling into an unbelieving condition that grieves and angers our Lord.

Our heavenly father wants us to be absolutely convinced from history that his promises to preserve his people always hold true, no matter what we face. It doesn't matter how dark the days become. The financial depression may grow deeper than our worst fears even allow. We may face scarcity to the point that we have to spend entire days on our knees, praying in our provision. Gross darkness may cover the earth. Yet, the fact remains, God will always preserve and protect his children. He wants us to know, "I've given you a whole Bible's worth of examples, to show you all the ways I've demonstrated my power on behalf of my people. You'll see lessons about my judgment, but you'll also see lessons about my provision. Just look back, study their history, and learn to trust me."

We must learn to heed the Lord's word on this matter. Otherwise, we'll spend our days as unbelieving Israel did, consumed by panic and grief!

Chapter Two

Biblical Prosperity in Hardship

A dear Christian man sent the following letter to me: "Pastor Wilkerson, for our whole lives, my wife and I have been good stewards of the blessings God has bestowed on us. We've supported many ministries like yours and of course our local congregation as well. We're grateful to the Lord that our investments have been good to us and now support us quite comfortably. My question to you is this: If the economy is about to collapse, where do you suggest we put our finances?

"Are we supposed to trust our mutual funds, or the stock market, or our local bank, or our bedroom mattress? It seems everyone sees the gloom ahead, but no one has any recommendations on how to prepare. My wife and I are out of debt, and we pay tithes faithfully, but we don't know what to do with the remainder of the money. What do you suggest? I know you're not a financial advisor, but you have us concerned. We'd love to hear from you and from the almighty."

A Christian couple from the Midwest wrote the following: "A Christian radio station in our area features prophetic teaching, and we've seen some strange reactions to the prophecies and warnings given during its programs. One man is determined to sell his house and move his family into an apartment because, he says, 'Things aren't going to last long anyway.' His wife is distressed, and their family is upset and disturbed over his decision. One church has closed down because the people have followed a certain prophetic word. There is so much misinterpreting of prophetic words going on."

A Christian brother from the West Coast wrote: "Our pension funds are invested in the stock market. As you know, pensions constitute the major source of income for countless Christians. A broad range of investments is dependent on the stock market, and most of us have no choice over the investing of our funds.

"Where should institutions be investing their endowment funds and annuities? If the market crashes, so will all the union pensions, teachers pensions, ministers pensions. I have a missionary calling, and I'll need these funds to survive. If any economic collapse is coming, we need solutions, answers."

These are just a few samples of the messages I've been hearing from sincere Christians all across the nation. The majority of these folks know that America's prosperity cannot last forever. They say, "How are we to prepare? Where is our ark of safety? Will God chasten his devoted children in the process of dealing with the wicked? Or, will he give us a clear word on how to invest the money we've earned honestly, so we can continue to support our families and his work through the coming storm?"

The people asking these questions are not rich, greedy Christians who are trying to hoard their money. Many are godly, praying, giving believers who want to be good stewards of what God has entrusted to them.

These Christians are saying, "We don't have any place to turn. We've been on our faces before the Lord, but we don't have any answers. Please, Pastor Wilkerson, give us something." Others are saying, "I live from paycheck to paycheck. I don't have any stocks or bonds, so this talk means nothing to me. I have to use all my resources just to pay my weekly and monthly bills. How am I going to make it if a depression comes?"

I believe God never hides any important matter from his precious children. If he's going to warn us about a coming storm, we can be sure he won't leave us living in constant fear and dread. No loving father treats his children that way, and our heavenly father is more loving than any. The truth is, he's ready and willing to supply us with his divine wisdom and guidance. Our problem is that we don't want to hear biblical, spiritual solutions. We want secular, worldly-wise answers to our problems such as whether to invest in gold, whether to switch our retirement funds, or whether to pour our savings into treasury notes.

Some people who've written to our ministry have been blunt enough to say what's really on their hearts. "Please, Pastor, don't give me some generic, spiritual pep talk about being led by a voice from God or about letting the Holy Spirit be my broker. I don't want to hear any more theological answers that say nothing about how I can find a safe haven for my savings. What does theology have to do with investments or knowing how to make it through hard times? I just want to know where to put my money."

One man wrote, "Way back in 1980 I asked God what he wanted me to do with our family's money. The scripture passage he directed me to started with the word 'money.' His word went on to say he was going to judge all nations of the earth for their continual sins. Within a week, the Lord told my wife in a dream we were to build a log home and live on five acres.

"I didn't move in this direction right away. In fact, it took us five years to move to the five acres. As confirmation, God did many unbelievable things – things we had no control over – to direct us to this point. We hope to start on the home by next spring.

"I believe without a doubt you are one of the godly men in this country, or at least I have that sense. I read with interest each of your newsletters. I am writing now to ask, how do we know this is the end? I felt back in 1980 we were close to the end. I've read the works of many other ministers who have believed the end was near. Over and over they have missed it, some because they were just trying to sell a book, others because they truly felt God was telling them this.

"Whom do we believe? If I had eliminated our family's investments way back then, we would have missed great opportunities. Does America stand at the same juncture now as I thought back in 1980? Or will we continue on the same way for many more years, possibly even decades?

"My parents have passed away, and they left us considerable stocks. Now it is my position to decide what should be done with these funds. If I remove them from the market, we'll have to pay a lot of taxes, and our Lord's judgment could still be many years away.

"I feel I have a responsibility to my children and grandchildren to help provide for them. If this is the great judgment on our country for all our unbelievable sins, then I would do well to take the money out, pay the taxes and ask God to show me where best to place the remainder for his and my family's use.

"This is an area of very large responsibility. It has taken several lifetimes for our family to accumulate this money. I have Christian friends who don't seem the least bit worried about any of this. In fact, I totally changed my investment thinking and remained out of programs that would have proven very good because of the knowledge of what God revealed to me in 1980. Had I known that the timetable was this long, though, I could have gone on. But we don't have that kind of knowledge available to us right now.

"Many people are making decisions based on their belief in your relationship with God. I am as well, giving this subject more consideration than I ever have before, because of what I believe about your walk with the Lord. And I believe the directive God gives each of his children should be very similar. If we are about to enter a time of major chaos, then that is knowledge the Lord would want each of his children to know. If the market is going to totally collapse, and we have food, water and medical shortages, then God would want each of us to know this as well. He may direct us individually to various areas of service, but on these major subjects we all should know the same thing. Why don't we? And how will we know when he is speaking to us?

"I am asking for more of an explanation than may be possible. I pray for each of us during this time, that we may be in God's will."

Many of my friends expect me to answer as an economist would. They want me to give them some hard-earned wisdom from my studies, some kind of "insider" advice I may have gotten in prayer. The fact is, I am not a prophet, and I don't know anything about economics.

But I have no doubt judgment is at the door because I've studied God's word on the matter. I realize that many people may not want to hear this, but I believe the most important thing we need to know right now is God's word. Sadly, multitudes of Christians have neglected their Bibles for so long and have had so little of God's pure word preached to them, they're no longer confident in what it has to say to them. They don't consider the scriptures their answer book anymore. Instead, they turn to the wisdom of the world. The Bible itself warns, "For it is written, I will destroy the wisdom of the wise, and will bring to nothing the understanding of the prudent... Hath not God made foolish the wisdom of this world?" (1 Corinthians 1:19-20).

Do I trust in an economist? No. Do I trust in financial newsletters written by unconverted economic wizards? No. Do I trust in mutual funds, stocks, bonds, money market investments, pension funds, Social Security? No. In short, I don't have confidence in any financial institution today. As Christians, we cannot put our trust in a financial institution, government agency or economist, when God says he's going to shake everything that can be shaken.

Isaiah prophesies, "They shall go into the holes of the rocks, and into the caves of the earth, for fear of the Lord, and for the glory of his majesty, when he ariseth to shake terribly the earth" (Isaiah 2:19). When God says, "I'm going to shake the whole world terribly," you'd better believe it's going to be an awesome shaking. The financial world is going to tremble violently beyond anything you could imagine.

I've heard many people say, "The only safe place to put money now is in U.S. Treasury bills." That is probably true, but even that kind of investment pays very little interest. I tell you, there are no more safe havens on this planet. The only solutions and answers are Bible solutions and spiritual answers, and I don't mean just some impractical theory.

The hard truth is this: If God is going to shake all things so that the only things left standing are those which can't be shaken, then we're to seek out those unshakable things and get on solid ground. I believe God's word clearly reveals what these unshakable things are. And he has given us an easily understood plan not only for how to survive, but for how to prosper in hard times.

There is a kind of believer who prospers in everything he does. God's word describes the prosperous believer this way: "He shall be like a tree planted by the rivers of water, that bringeth forth his fruit in his season; his leaf also shall not wither; and whatsoever he doeth shall prosper" (Psalm 1:3). The word "prosper" here means "to overcome all adversity" or "to go over adversities." In the words of the psalmist, this believer is going to overcome, whether his adversities are spiritual, physical or economic.

In contrast, David says, "The ungodly are not so: but are like the chaff which the wind driveth away" (Psalm 1:4). According to Jesus, the storm that's coming will panic the wicked, driving them to despair. He foresaw "men's hearts failing them for fear, and for looking after those things which are coming on the earth: for the powers of heaven shall be shaken" (Luke 21:26).

Yet the godly will not be driven to despair. They're going to face the same violent winds of calamity, the same awful times, but they'll prosper in spirit. Through it all, they'll still be doing good works, spiritually prospering and overcoming, even in the worst of times. This is God's measure of prosperity, although it isn't the kind that's recognized or sought by the world. It doesn't consist of wealth, possessions or hoarded assets. Instead, it includes peace, comfort and provision and the absence of fear and terror when the world begins to shake.

The New York Times reported that a number of wealthy people in New York City have "golden parachutes" – that is, their plan of escape – in place for when the storm hits. They've bought retreats in the country, and they've stockpiling them with food, supplies and even guns. Their chauffeurs are on alert, waiting to scoot them out of the city at the first sign of rioting or violence.

When the Lord begins pulling down every trusted institution in America and panic hits the nation, though, the only real wealth left will be the knowledge of the Lord Jesus Christ and his ways. All true security rests in him. Only by being in him can we have the peace of knowing that no matter what calamities fall, no wind or storm will be able to blow us away.

The Christian who is prosperous in hard times is the one who has given up on the counsel of the ungodly, and who has cast himself on the word of God as his only guide.

David says of the prosperous believer, "Blessed is the man that walketh not in the counsel of the ungodly, nor standeth in the way of sinners, nor sitteth in the seat of the scornful" (Psalm 1:1). The psalmist is speaking about much more than a righteous person's being enticed to indulge in abominable lusts, or to go to wicked places with evil companions, or to associate with godless mockers. David is talking about where we seek our advice and get our counsel. This verse is saying, "Blessed is the believer who refuses to make decisions, or invest, or be influenced by the counsel of ungodly experts who hold God's word in derision."

David then describes the behavior of this prosperous believer. "His delight is in the law of the Lord; and in his law doth he meditate day and night" (Psalm 1:2). In essence, he's saying, "If you want to be prepared, you're going to have to forsake all your dependence on secular thinking. God will not allow his bride to depend on anyone or anything of this world. His followers are to have the mind of his son. And, like Jesus, they're to seek the father with all their heart, soul, mind and strength."

At this point, you may be thinking, "Pastor, your message is trickery; it's deceptive. First, you lead us to believe we can prosper in hard times, then you refuse to give us any sound advice on how to go about prospering. Instead, you fall back on nebulous concepts like, 'Just trust God,' and, 'Trust your Bible.' That's old stuff to us. And it's not practical at all. I need to know where I can put my money, how to prepare, how to act wisely, how to survive!"

I tell you, these "spiritual" answers are the very heart of the matter, and nothing else is truly important until that is settled. Turning to the Lord has everything to do with being preserved in hard times, and it has everything to do with practicality. In fact, it is the only way to prepare and to survive. It's the first step, the place where each of us must begin. After all, we can't expect God to give us direction if we don't go to him and ask for it.

God will not allow his people to go anywhere but to him for counsel and direction. Any placing of confidence in the ungodly who scoff at his word is considered wickedness. God's word is not vague at all on this issue of turning to the counsel of the ungodly.

"Woe to them that go down to Egypt for help; and stay on horses, and trust in chariots, because they are many; and in horsemen, because they are very strong; but they look not unto the Holy One of Israel, neither seek the Lord!" (Isaiah 31:1). Isaiah was saying to God's people, "You're running everywhere looking for direction. You want counsel. You want advice, but you won't come to the Lord!"

The prophet warns that all confidence in ungodly help will ultimately fail. "...they all shall fail together" (Isaiah 31:3). Jeremiah gives a similarly blunt warning: "Thus saith the Lord; Cursed be the man that trusteth in man, and maketh flesh his arm, and whose heart departeth from the Lord" (Jeremiah 17:5).

Then Jeremiah adds this word of hope: "Blessed is the man that trusteth in the Lord, and whose hope the Lord is. For he shall be as a tree planted by the waters, and that spreadeth out her roots by the river, and shall not see when heat cometh, but her leaf shall be green; and shall not be careful in the year of drought, neither shall cease from yielding fruit" (Jeremiah 17:7-8).

Those who fully trust in the Lord Jesus Christ need not be moved at all by looking into the future. Of course, none of us knows the full extent of the awful storm we're going to face, but that doesn't matter to those whose faith is anchored in God's word.

We see an illustration of this kind of faith in the life of the apostle Paul. He wrote, "And now, behold, I go bound in the spirit unto Jerusalem, not knowing the things that shall befall me there" (Acts 20:22). As Paul was on his way to Jerusalem, he had no idea what would happen to him. He didn't know he would be dragged out of the temple by a wild mob; that the city would get into an uproar over him, upset by his teachings; that he would be bound with chains, jailed and threatened with death; that he would be brought before rulers, tried and examined; and that he would finally end up in a Roman prison. Yet, no matter what lay ahead, Paul could testify sincerely, "As I look into the future, I have no idea what's coming for me down the road. All I know is, the Holy Ghost has warned me that hard times and afflictions are ahead." "...the Holy Ghost witnesseth in every city, saying that bonds and afflictions abide me" (Acts 20:23).

Why was Paul ready to face any hardship or danger that lay ahead? He knew the Holy Ghost was faithful to warn him beforehand. Although he knew perilous times were just around the bend, Paul could say, "But none of these things move me, neither count I my life dear unto myself..." (Acts 20:24). This man of God testified to the whole world: "Hard times, perilous times, times of shakings – none of these things bother me. I'm not holding onto anything, even my very life. It can all go, because I get no pleasure from anything in this world. I value nothing but Christ. He is my only reality. That's why I'm dying daily to this world. Good times, bad times, abounding times, abasing times – they're all the same to me. None of these things matters, because I have Christ. He is my everything! My Christ will carry me through every hard time. He will make a way."

One reason Paul wasn't moved by potential hardships was because he didn't covet wealth or possessions. On the contrary, he knew that whatever he had was to be shared with the poor and needy. "I have coveted no man's silver, or gold, or apparel...I have shewed you all things, how that so labouring ye ought to support the weak, and to remember the words of the Lord Jesus, how he said, It is more blessed to give than to receive" (Acts 20:33, 35).

I witnessed this same godly attitude in a letter our ministry received from a wonderful Christian grandmother.

This woman believes God has shown her in prayer that times will get so bad, many people won't be able to get even the small things they need. As a result, she has begun collecting needles, matches, candles, thread, hairpins, etc. – all the things people normally throw away. She now has rooms full of these things she's been saving. Why? She wants to be able to bless people, to give to the poor and needy in hard times.

Now, contrast her spirit with those people – including some Christians – who are determined to protect their stored food supply with guns. I've seen books on how to prepare for the coming depression, and many of them have a totally militant spirit. Some authors, including believers, suggest that people should be prepared to protect their supplies at all costs, even if it means shooting intruders.

Of course, it is wise to store some food and supplies but only on the condition of Paul's instruction: "Support the weak. Share what you have, rather than hoarding it all for yourself."

Let me tell you why none of these coming calamities should move us because our hour of darkness is Christ's hour of power.

God's hour of power is revealed when his people are brought to the end of their own strength and ability. Our Lord demonstrates his power toward us when we're at our lowest point.

A wonderful example of this is found in the gospel of John. Jesus, his mother and his disciples were invited to a marriage feast in Cana. You know the story: When the wedding party ran out of wine, Mary turned to Jesus and said, "Son, they don't have any more wine. Please, do something." But Jesus answered, "...Woman, what have I to do with thee? Mine hour is not yet come" (John 2:4).

Now, Christ's response to his mother here was not one of disrespect. In fact, in oriental culture, to address a mother as "woman" was the highest order of respect. Jesus was literally saying, "Mother, I can't do what you're asking. It's not quite my time yet." This was in keeping with Christ's commitment to do only what his heavenly father showed him to do.

We know, however, that Jesus' hour came shortly after this conversation. That's when he did change water into wine for the wedding guests. Indeed, this was "the hour" for his demonstration of power. But why did Jesus at first say his hour had not yet come?

I believe it was because when Mary first spoke to him, the people at the wedding still had wine in their cups. Christ was telling his mother, "My time for demonstrating my power hasn't arrived, because these people haven't yet run completely out of their resources. My hour comes when there's no hope left, when there are no remaining resources to depend on in the flesh. It has to be a moment of total dependence on me. And right now, for me to demonstrate my power, every bottle and cup has to be empty, dry. There can be nothing left in a single cup before I become these people's provider. All resources have to be exhausted."

That's the time when Christ moves in with power, when all our resources have dried up. This is exactly what happened with God's people at the Red Sea. Israel cried out for God to show his power against their enemy, the Egyptians. But God waited until all hope in human deliverance was gone and all man-made plans were exhausted. Only in that darkest hour did God move.

So it is in the lives of God's people today. Our Lord's hour comes when we see there is nothing we can do to change our circumstances. It happens when we realize, "I don't know where my paycheck is going to come from. I don't know what's going to happen to me or my family. I don't see any resource on either the left or the right. Humanly speaking, there's nothing on the horizon to bring me any reassurance. I do not know where to invest, or what to do about my finances. But I have his promise to display his power to keep and preserve me and my family."

Christ's demonstration of power in this passage was not meant merely to please the wedding guests, or to save the bridal party from embarrassment. His miraculous work was intended to increase the faith of those in his inner circle, his disciples. The lesson he taught them applies to us today. He's saying, "I want you to see that my first love is my people. I care that you have enough to eat, that you have a roof over your heads, that you have clothing. When everything around you collapses, that is my hour to demonstrate to you my powerful love and care for you!"

The whole earth is about to come under the cover of gross darkness, an hour of such deprivation and confusion that only Christ can meet our needs in it. We may run out of all resources, with no human power to turn to for help. Yet we can find comfort and assurance in this biblical truth: the darker things get, the brighter our Lord's light will shine. Our time of desperation is our Lord's hour of power, and he will provide.

You may worry, "Will there be a depression? Will a stock market crash be followed by unemployment, exhausted food resources, uncertainty, darkness everywhere?" My only answer is this: Hold fast to your faith, and know that Christ's hour of power has come. Yes, we may be facing the greatest hour of darkness in history. But this also means we're going to witness the greatest miracles of any past generation. When all our resources are exhausted, we'll see miracle after miracle of provision, with God performing supernatural wonders. He's saving the best wine for these last days – and he's going to miraculously see to it that our daily supply will not be exhausted.

Thank God, the light in that darkest hour is going to rise in our hearts, and it's going to shine brighter than ever!

Chapter Three

Preparing for Hard Times

Numerous Christian investment advisors have circulated different information about how believers can prepare for perilous times. The most common advice they offer is for people to move out of the cities, buy land in secluded areas, dig wells, provide for storage and start hoarding food, blankets and supplies in order to have a two- to three-year supply on hand for a major financial crisis.

An elderly Christian woman was given this advice by her friends, who were acting on it themselves. Not long ago, this dear woman wrote to our ministry, asking, "Pastor David, what can I do to prepare for the hard times coming? I'm eighty-seven years and four months old, with limited funds. It's impossible for me to do all the things they're telling me I need to do to prepare. I would deeply love to live in the country and have my own well water. I was brought up on a farm, and I know what it's like to live without modern conveniences. I was one of twelve children. And I've always kept a good supply of food on hand, the way I learned growing up. But I still put my trust in God first, and I pray to him for direction. What else shall I do to prepare?"

I'm writing this chapter for that dear, 87-year-old saint and for all other Christians living in cities and towns who have limited incomes, who live from paycheck to paycheck, who have no money to buy hideaways, and yet who want to be fully prepared for economic down-turns. Let me give you what I believe is God's mind on this matter of preparing for hard times. I want to show you how to prepare his way, not man's way. You don't need a huge cash reserve, and you don't need to leave your apartment or house and relocate to the country (unless the Lord has led you to do so). God already has a plan for you.

I sought the Lord diligently about my responsibility to my congregation at Times Square Church in New York City. I prayed for weeks about what I should do to prepare them for difficult days ahead. One day I took a walk along a quiet country road, so I could be alone with the Lord to discern his voice. I started my walk at about dusk, and there was a bright moon overhead.

A few years before the Gulf War, I warned there would be five hundred fires burning in the Middle East. Most people winked at my words. After the war, there were precisely five hundred and three fires consuming Kuwaiti oil wells, all set aflame by Saddam Hussein. That and many other warnings I've received have come to pass. So these days I listen intently when the Lord is speaking to me about coming events.

On the country road that night, I was seeing in my mind's eye New York City burning in flames. I saw more than a thousand fires burning at one time, an image I had seen before. There were riots, bloodshed, tanks rolling into the streets, troops wielding rifles in an attempt to restore order. People were mobbing grocery stores for provisions, looting merchants, raging out of control.

As I walked farther along, I thought of all the wonder-ful, faithful people who attend Times Square Church, devoted Christians who could be caught in the middle of it all. I became so overwhelmed that I had to grab onto a rail fence to support myself.

I started weeping, crying out to the Lord, "Oh, God, how can I prepare these devoted people for such devastation? They all can't just pick up everything and flee the city. Most have no car, no transportation and little income. They struggle just to pay rent and buy subway tokens, much less to buy hideaways in Vermont or Montana.

"They have no family outside the city, no hiding place, very little space to lay up supplies for emergencies. Most live in cramped apartments that are already overcrowded with the bare essentials. Please, Father, give us a word. What can I do as a pastor? You've told me to warn them about what's coming. Why can't you give me your plan for preserving us? What do you want me to tell your people?"

The Lord heard my cry, and he gave me a comforting word. He whispered to my heart, "David, you're seeing this whole matter from your point of view. Let me show you mine."

Here is what I believe is God's plan for his people's survival, in any and all storms.

The only trustworthy preparations are those for the heart, not the body. If you love the Lord, this is where all preparations must begin. This subject of preparation is primarily a spiritual matter and only secondarily one of bodily or material concern. If your heart is not right with the Lord, all your preparations to protect your body will be in vain.

Those who right now are setting their hearts to seek God with all their being — saturating their hearts and minds with his word and cleaving to Christ more and more — are better prepared for the coming storm than anyone. They're safer and more protected than even those Christians who have stored away a year or two's supply of food in some country haven but have not focused on their spiritual well-being.

Now let me prove all this to you from scripture.

When God told the children of Israel to prepare to leave Egypt at any moment, he didn't give them instructions about how to stockpile food, water or supplies for their journey, though I see nothing wrong in doing those things. Instead, he told Moses, "Just stand by." Talk about facing hard times. These people were headed into a wilderness — a barren, waterless desert — with no visible resources whatsoever. They faced zero employment with no store of supplies and no source of water. At least in Egypt they had all the food they needed, but now the only thing they had was a promise from God to support and preserve them as they made their way through the desert.

The only instructions God gave Israel for preparation were spiritual in nature, all preparations of the heart. In brief, the Lord told them three things:

1. "Get secured by the blood."

Each family was to kill a lamb and sprinkle the animal's blood on the doorpost of their home, and they were told to rest securely in that blood. As long as the lamb's blood was applied to the doorpost, that family remained safe from the Lord's avenging angel who was about to strike Egypt. So, by heeding God's instructions, the Israelites were secure not only spiritually but also physically. Under the lamb's blood, everyone in the home remained safe.

The parallels for us today are clear. We're to prepare for coming calamities by making sure we're under the blood of the lamb, Jesus Christ. We're to put our confidence in the delivering power of his shed blood and to rest securely in that by faith.

2. "Eat the lamb."

The Israelites were to feast on the lamb that was slain. Of course, the lamb they ate was a type of Christ. The slain animal represented his slain body and shed blood. Likewise today, as we face the coming hard times, we're reminded by this passage to feed on Christ, just as the Israelites feasted on the lamb by God's instruction.

Let me ask you, what are you feasting on these days? Are you building up your spiritual body by feeding your soul with his promises and by having times of intimacy with him? Are you digesting God's word daily, hiding his word in your heart? Are you growing spiritually strong to face the wilderness experience before you, when all human resources fail? If not, you'd better start feasting on him now, while there is still time. He's the food you should be storing up.

3. "Be ready to go at any time."

Israel was to be prepared to leave everything behind at a moment's notice, to forsake all that was comfortable and secure. When the time finally came for them to leave, the only food they had with them was unleavened dough. It was just enough to last them a few days. The Lord instructed them, "You're going to have to learn to trust me, to cast your welfare and future completely into my hands."

The same is true for us today. We're not to be tied down

to anything in this world. Rather, we have to be prepared to trust our very lives into God's care in a way we've never before realized. We're to have a new Jerusalem state of mind with our eyes fixed on eternity. We have to be prepared to lose everything and to trust our lives, families and futures into our Lord's caring hands completely.

We see this kind of preparation illustrated in scripture, in the image of the bride of Christ. God has chosen us, his overcoming church, as a bride for his son. This bride is spoken for, set apart, engaged to be wed to Jesus, "...which he hath purchased with his own blood" (Acts 20:28).

What should be the focus of this bride? Her sole focus ought to be to prepare herself for the wedding, to ready herself to be with her beloved. I believe God's heart grieves over the poor spiritual condition of his son's bride. Sadly, many who comprise the bride of Christ have eyes for other lovers. They have corrupted themselves by loving this world and its things, and now their bridal garments have become soiled and stained.

The apostle Paul writes, "...even as Christ also loved the church, and gave himself for it; that he might sanctify and cleanse it with the washing of water by the word, that he might present it to himself a glorious church, not having spot, or wrinkle, or any such thing; but that it should be holy and without blemish" (Ephesians 5:25-27). Paul makes it very plain, "We are to be holy for our bridegroom without spot, wrinkle or blemish!"

We're supposed to be making preparations to leave this sin-cursed world to be with Jesus, not clinging to more and more things of this world. You are not truly a lover of Jesus if you are not daily preparing to meet him!

In the book of Revelation, we read of a holy people coming down from God out of heaven, prepared as a bride.

"And I John saw the holy city, new Jerusalem, coming down from God out of heaven, prepared as a bride adorned for her husband" (Revelation 21:2). The holy city John is talking about here is Zion, and it's made up of the overcoming, spiritual children of God. These people are seated with Christ in heavenly places. They spend much time alone with their Lord, seeking his face. Every time they emerge from their secret closet of prayer, they are, as John says, "coming down from God out of heaven" where they've spent time with him.

This "bride company" of believers gets no pleasure from this world. Their affections are not set on material things; rather, their hearts are always where their Lord is. They may be relatively few in number, but they have eyes for no one but Jesus. He has a magnetic pull on their hearts that draws them to his presence. Every morning they get up thinking, "Lord, I thank you for my family, my job and all that you've provided, but I know nothing of this earth is going to last. My heart isn't here. It's with you, Jesus!"

The saints who make up the overcoming bride of Christ today aren't preparing to save their skin in a storm. The most important preparation they're making is to leave for a great wedding feast. This bride is adorning herself, readying herself, purifying herself by faith. She's setting her heart in order, allowing it to be drawn to her beloved. Her heart is no longer attached to anything of this world, because she only wants to be with her bridegroom.

What a wonderful, heavenly image of the work going on in Jesus' bride on earth. Yet I wonder how many other Christians are more seriously at work making arrangements to provide for their physical well-being. Their whole focus is on getting everything in order to ride out the financial storm. They aren't feasting on the lamb; instead, they're stressed out trying to beat the storm. They're besotting their hearts with the filth of this world, because they've made earthly matters their focus. Now they're no longer a spiritual people but a sensual one.

There must be great grief in heaven over these multitudes who pour their energies into making sure their earthly destiny is secure. Our Lord must be saying, "Oh, that you could give me that kind of intensity, that you could make such intricate preparations in your heart for me!"

I'm not against those who warn Christians to prepare for calamity by taking physical precautions. On the surface, it makes sense to have a supply of food and water on hand and to take any other precautions God leads you to take. Many who preach this kind of preparation are believers who quote a verse in Proverbs, "A prudent man foreseeth the evil, and hideth himself: but the simple pass on, and are punished" (Proverbs 22:3). These believers claim that because this same verse is repeated later, in Proverbs 27:12, it must be important to act on it, and that is true.

I believe, though, this passage applies even more to spiritual preparation than to physical. Using similar language, Isaiah writes, "A man shall be as an hiding place from the wind, and a covert from the tempest; as rivers of water in a dry place, as the shadow of a great rock in a weary land" (Isaiah 32:2). The "man" Isaiah is talking about here is Christ. He's saying, in essence, "If you're prudent and wise, you'll get secure under Christ's blood. You'll hide yourself in him, set your faith on him and place all your confidence in him."

Many believers have put their eternal destiny into the

Lord's hands, but not all have done the same with their earthly destiny. If the only preparation you're making for the future is for your personal security, you're headed for very difficult times. Think about it. How much can you stockpile and for how long? It makes good sense to have a few months' supply of food, but what if you store up goods for a year or two, and the hard times last three? Some economists predict that the economic nightmare we're headed for may last for a very long time, and I agree with them. So what if it lasts eight, ten, twelve years, or even more?

There simply is no possible failsafe way to prepare for what's coming. Of course, God will direct his people concerning what to do, how to act wisely and how to lay aside what will be needed. But that should never be the focus of Christ's bride.

I assure you, if you're making spiritual preparations – getting your heart in order, dealing with sin, calling on the Lord with greater intensity, trusting in his word, building up your faith – then you're readying yourself for anything. You'll be able to face a depression, losses and privations, calamities all around. You'll be ready for all troubled waters, floods, fiery furnaces, persecution, crop failures, droughts, shortages, sicknesses. Most of all, you'll be ready to hear the trumpet of God in the last hour. You'll be prepared to march into the wedding feast to be united with Christ.

God has made a covenant to keep and protect those who stay passionately in love with him.

I believe the covenant God has made with us holds the secret to perfect peace, no matter what storm may come. He first made this covenant with Abraham. Scripture tells us: "...the word of the Lord came unto Abram in a vision, saying, Fear not, Abram: I am thy shield, and thy exceeding great reward" (Genesis 15:1). The word "shield" in this verse means "protector, hedge, wall of security." What an amazing promise! God was assuring Abraham, "No matter where you go, and no matter what you face, you never have to be afraid. I'm all you'll ever need."

In addition, the phrase "exceeding great reward" here means, literally, "salary, wages, compensation, benefits." God was telling Abraham, in so many words, "I'm not only going to protect you, but I'll also take care of your physical needs. I'll be your guide, your paymaster. Everything you receive will come from my hand. All you have to do is walk righteously before me, put your trust in me and love me with all your heart. If you do these things, I'll compensate you with all the necessities in your daily life."

God also made this covenant with Abraham's son, Isaac, and with Isaac's son, Jacob, and then with all of Israel. Finally, it was made to all of the "seed of Abraham." Of course, Abraham's seed consists of all who live and abide in Christ Jesus, walking in faith in his redeeming blood. "...They which are the children of the flesh, these are not the children of God: but the children of the promise are counted for the seed [of Abraham]" (Romans 9:8). "Know ye therefore that they which are of faith, the same are the children of Abraham" (Galatians 3:7). If you daily trust Jesus as your Lord and savior, resting in him by faith, then you are the seed of Abraham.

You may ask, "What's so important about being the seed of Abraham? Why should I be so concerned over this matter?" It's important because God made this everlasting covenant to be a shield, a protector, a wall of security with Abraham and his seed. As Abraham's children, we are to claim this covenant by faith. We're to lay claim to the same power, deliverance and protection God promised to Abraham. Because God made a vow to keep Abraham's seed by his grace and power, no believer ever has to be afraid again.

Certainly, this covenant reaches us today. The Bible says, "He hath remembered his covenant for ever, the word which he commanded to a thousand generations. Which covenant he made with Abraham, and his oath unto Isaac" (Psalm 105:8-9). "And confirmed the same unto Jacob for a law, and to Israel for an everlasting covenant" (Psalm 105:10).

What greater protection could we have, than to be under God's covenant oath to keep us and supply our every need in the hardest of times? All we have to do in return is love him. Listen again to God's word on the matter.

"I call heaven and earth to record this day against you, that I have set before you life and death, blessing and cursing: therefore choose life, that both thou and thy seed may live: that thou mayest love the Lord thy God, and that thou mayest obey his voice, and that thou mayest cleave unto him: for he is thy life, and the length of thy days: that thou mayest dwell in the land which the Lord sware unto thy fathers, to Abraham, to Isaac, and to Jacob, to give them" (Deuteronomy 30:19-20).

God assures us here, as he assured Israel, "It doesn't matter what happens all around you. I will bless you with enough. I will be your security!"

After reading and hearing of God's covenant to protect his people, many Christians are still unable to deal with a certain Bible passage.

Many Christians believe the following scripture passage goes directly against all of God's covenant promises: "Others had trial of cruel mockings and scourgings, yea, moreover of bonds and imprisonment: they were stoned, they were sawn asunder, were tempted, were slain with the sword: they wandered about in sheepskins and goatskins; being destitute, afflicted, tormented; (of whom the world was not worthy:) they wandered in deserts, and in mountains, and in dens and caves of the earth. And these all, having obtained a good report through faith, received not the promise: God having provided some better thing for us, that they without us should not be made perfect" (Hebrews 11:36-40).

Some believers who read this passage can't help wondering, "Where was the protection for these martyred believers? Where was the wall, the hedge? They all loved Christ passionately. They had to, to be martyred for him."

We've got to accept the fact that there's going to be a lot more terrible suffering in the body of Christ until Jesus comes. John writes of those who will be martyred, "When he had opened the fifth seal, I saw under the altar the souls of them that were slain for the word of God, and for the testimony which they held: and they cried with a loud voice, saying, 'How long, O Lord, holy and true, dost thou not judge and avenge our blood on them that dwell on the earth?' And white robes were given unto every one of them; and it was said unto them, that they should rest yet for a little season, until their fellow servants also and their brethren, that should be killed as they were, should be fulfilled" (Revelation 6:9-11).

Here is a sober warning to Christ's church. Many believers are going to be slain for their Lord's sake, right up to the very end.

Of course, none of us wants to hear this kind of news, but we can be sure it will happen, just as scripture says. I saw an example of this kind of suffering recently in a missions report I received. The report told of the horrible persecution of Chinese Christians in Indonesia. Secular news agencies have reported on the riots in which these Chinese people were killed, but the reports didn't mention that many were killed because of their Christian faith. More than 1,500 were brutally murdered, and many women were raped.

Those people mentioned in Hebrews and Revelation, who submitted to horrible sufferings, were a chosen people who were very special to the Lord. I believe they clung to Christ so intensely that their hearts were already in glory with him. They surely must have rejoiced over anything that would provide them a quick route to his side.

Scripture testifies these were "...slain for the word of God, and for the testimony which they held" (Revelation 6:9). It didn't matter to these saints whether they lived or died. Even if God didn't deliver them from death, they weren't going to compromise their testimony. The Bible says they even chose not to be delivered and instead received a "better resurrection."

I believe this kind of martyrdom is reserved for a special people. As the author of Hebrews writes, the world simply isn't worthy of their kind. Martyrdom is a special calling for a chosen people.

Yet we who probably won't be martyred should take heart. God loves the faint-hearted like you and me just as much as he loves those who are killed for their faith. Our Lord has enough servants who are willing to submit to the high honor of suffering for him even unto death; he doesn't have to call on the cowardly or fearful, and his covenant still stands for all of his children. His promises are still true!

Even if we do eventually face persecution and death, our Lord will give us all the grace we need in the hour we need it. As we go to meet him, we'll know the most blessed experience of our existence. We'll go out shouting God's praises because we will have been gloriously surprised and prepared by his grace.

This is God's promise to deliver us, being fulfilled in a way that brings us quickly into his presence and glory. There is nothing to fear!

CHAPTER FOUR

THE PRESERVATION OF ZION

Jesus said perilous times would come, frightening times of chaos and calamity. Beyond these terrible crises, though, there is good news for God's holy people, hopeful, exciting news. I believe once we lay hold of this news, we won't have to worry about understanding any of the coming events or knowing the details of what's ahead. Instead, we'll be able to rest and enjoy total peace because of the word God gives us.

Even as I write this, a number of prophecy conferences are taking place all over the world, drawing multitudes of Christians. Many of these believers are literally addicted to knowing the latest theories on events prophesied in scripture. In the end, though, trying to figure out the many prophetic events will only send people running in circles.

I don't believe any Christian is meant to get a single moment of peace from knowing precisely what's to come.

Jesus himself says we're not supposed to fear any future event, no matter how devastating it may appear. He says, "When these things begin to come to pass, then look up, and lift up your heads; for your redemption draweth nigh" (Luke 21:28).

I believe we're to take Christ's words on this subject

literally. We're to seek the Lord alone to find hope for his church in these last days.

Moreover, I'm convinced all we need to know about the evil day to come is summed up in one simple truth. God has made an ironclad promise to protect and preserve Zion. Who is Zion? In this chapter, I want to show you that Zion is the overcoming church of Jesus Christ, and that God's "Zion promises" belong to us who believe. Then I want to show you some of the incredible promises of deliverance and preservation God has given to Zion.

Scripture reveals that Zion – as Israel was sometimes called in the Old Testament – is the last-days church, a people of God who are blood-bought and walking in the righteousness of Christ, whether Jew or Gentile. In short, if you're in Christ, then you're a citizen of this spiritual nation called Zion.

However, not all Bible teachers and preachers believe this. Some say Zion represents only the city of David in ancient Israel, a specific geographical location that existed at a particular time and nothing more. Therefore, these teachers assert, the promises God makes to Zion are Old Testament truths that don't relate at all to the church today but only to the nation of Israel under the Old Covenant.

Yet both the Old and New Testaments make clear that there are two Zions or Israels, a natural Israel on earth and a spiritual Israel. We see this truth demonstrated in the Old Testament through Jacob's two names – his natural, fleshly name, Jacob, and his regenerate, spiritual name, Israel. We also see two Zions, or Israels, mentioned in the New Testament. One of these is an "Israel after the flesh," according to Paul (see 1 Corinthians 10:18). This refers to the literal nation of Israel, people who are Jewish by virtue of birth, natural lineage and ethnic heritage. By contrast, Paul says, there is another Israel that he calls "the Israel of God" (Galatians 6:16). The Jews referred to here couldn't be just natural Jews because in this context Paul is speaking of a people who had become new creatures in Christ (see Galatians 6:15). To underscore this difference, Paul writes, "For they are not all Israel, which are of Israel" (Romans 9:6). This is to say, not everyone who's literally born into the nation of Israel is one of God's spiritual children.

Remember what Paul says. "...They which are the children of the flesh, these are not the children of God: but the children of the promise are counted for the seed [of Abraham]" (Romans 9:8). Only those who come to God by faith in Christ are truly the children of Abraham. We see a type of this in the life of Jacob, who received his regenerate, or spiritual, name "Israel" only by faith in God's grace. "Know ye therefore that they which are of faith, the same are the children of Abraham" (Galatians 3:7). The children of Abraham are those who by faith have received Jesus Christ as king and Lord in their lives. God makes special promises to this "spiritual seed" of Abraham that are not promised to the natural seed.

We also see references to two Zions in regard to the city of Jerusalem. The New Testament word for "Jerusalem" is a form of "Zion" spelled "Sion." This Jerusalem has nothing to do with the city located in the Middle East. Rather, Paul writes, "This Agar is mount Sinai in Arabia, and answereth to Jerusalem which now is, and is in bondage with her children. But Jerusalem which is above is free, which is the mother of us all" (Galatians 4:25-26).

Followers of Jesus belong to this other Jerusalem, the

spiritual Jerusalem. The Bible says this new Jerusalem is a heavenly one, populated by those who are born into its citizenship by faith in Christ: "...I will write upon him the name of my God, and the name of the city of my God, which is new Jerusalem, which cometh down out of heaven from my God..." (Revelation 3:12). If you're a Christian, then you are a spiritual Jew, a citizen of Zion.

According to the psalmist, "Of Zion it shall be said, This and that man was born in her: and the highest himself shall establish her. The Lord shall count, when he writeth up the people, that this man was born there" (Psalm 87:5-6). Ultimately, this nation is not my home. I thank God for my American heritage, and I'm patriotic about my homeland. But my home is in spiritual Zion, the new Jerusalem. And I can get there only by being born again in Jesus Christ. God has made me a "Zionian" by faith!

Isaiah gives us proof positive that Zion is comprised of a spiritual people. He writes, "Zion shall be redeemed with judgment, and her converts with righteousness" (Isaiah 1:27). We know all righteousness is wrapped up in Christ. When we were born again by faith in him, we were made citizens of Zion by his righteousness.

In addition, Isaiah says Zion shall be called "The city of the Lord, The Zion of the Holy One of Israel...I will make thee an eternal excellency..." (Isaiah 60:14-15). An "eternal city" cannot be a natural city, such as the literal Jerusalem in Israel because the Bible says all of natural creation is going to burn. The only city that can truly be called eternal is the city of God, and that city is spiritual Zion.

Please understand, however, this spiritual Zion is not merely heaven. We are not just marching to Zion, as the hymn says because we're already living there. Zion is the overcoming church of Jesus Christ alive and well on the planet earth, consisting of believers from all nations, kindreds and tongues, born-again Jews and Gentiles. We comprise the city of our great God, the mountain of his holiness, the joy of the whole earth.

Finally, because there are two kinds of Zion, there are also two kinds of Jews: Jews of the flesh and spiritual Jews. Paul says the spiritual Jew is recognized as the recipient of God's Zion promises. He writes, "For he is not a Jew, which is one outwardly; neither is that circumcision, which is outward in the flesh: but he is a Jew, which is one inwardly; and circumcision is that of the heart, in the spirit, and not in the letter; whose praise is not of men, but of God" (Romans 2:28-29).

Because of the work of Christ, this "spiritual Jew" can receive the glorious promises of God. Of course, natural Israel still has its covenants of future blessings, but all of those blessings still depend on returning to the true Messiah, Jesus Christ. (No true Christian gives up hope for natural Israel. God still has a plan of restoration for the Zion of the flesh.)

Let me stop at this point and reassure you. All this talk of spiritual Zion, spiritual Israel, spiritual Jerusalem and spiritual Jews isn't some fanciful interpretation of biblical truth. It isn't just a theological supposition or a doctrinal scheme. Rather, God intends it for us as foundational truth by which to live. By making us his spiritual Zion, he desires that we never again have to wonder, "How is God going to take care of me during the perilous times to come? How will he protect my family from the financial holocaust? How is he going to preserve his church when everything begins to fall apart?" We're about to receive our answer to all these questions through all of God's promises to Zion.

Let me list for you some of the many promises God has made to protect and preserve Zion. If you're a born-again citizen of Zion, each of the following promises is yours.

God promises to provide a covering and a defense for Zion through every storm and crisis.

The psalmist writes, "God is known in her [Zion's] palaces for a refuge" (Psalm 48:3). Isaiah writes, "The Lord will create upon every dwelling place of mount Zion, and upon her assemblies, a cloud and smoke by day, and the shining of a flaming fire by night: for upon all the glory shall be a defense. And there shall be a tabernacle for a shadow in the daytime from the heat, and for a place of refuge, and for a covert from storm and from rain" (Isaiah 4:5-6).

In these passages, God is telling us, "I'm going to make known to every home in Zion — small or large, rich or poor — that if you'll simply trust me, I will be your refuge." In Zion, God promises, "You will never again have to flee or run!"

The Lord wants us to know that even when our cities' streets and rural highways are packed with cars bumper to bumper, trying to flee, we won't have anything to fear. "Thus saith the Lord God, Behold, I lay in Zion for a foundation a stone, a tried stone, a precious corner stone, a sure foundation: he that believeth shall not make haste" (Isaiah 28:16). What a wonderful promise God makes to us here: "Because of what I have done for you, you won't have to flee in haste, not to the mountains, not to the deserts, not to the countryside. I will be with you!"

God made this promise to his people in a time when dreadful judgments were falling all over the land. Israel's fat, prosperous society was fading like dying flowers. And now a destroying storm had suddenly come upon the land as an "overflowing scourge," sweeping away all lies and hypocrisy. People were fleeing in all directions, seeking hiding places of any kind. But God's righteous remnant was safe in Zion, settled on a rock.

If you're in Zion, then you've found your hiding place, your refuge. All who follow Christ, resting in his faithfulness and trusting in his care, need never run in fear. He is a rock not only to those who live in the quiet, relatively safe countryside but also to those in the middle of the city. "They that trust in the Lord shall be as mount Zion, which cannot be removed, but abideth for ever" (Psalm 125:1).

At some point, the mayor of New York City proposed that the city spend $15 to $20 million to build a deep, underground command center for city officials and police to convene in the event of a major catastrophe. The command center would have to be dug out of rock, on which the island of Manhattan sits. In the mayor's mind, it would provide the ultimate safety to the city's leaders.

Yet even this kind of refuge – apparently the best man-made shelter available – can never compare to the safety of the rock shelter of Zion. Moses says, "Their rock is not as our Rock, even our enemies themselves being judges" (Deuteronomy 32:31). When God begins his shaking, every man-made refuge is going to tremble; but Zion's rock cannot be shaken because it is Christ himself. He is a rock that has been tested and tried and remains a sure foundation.

God has promised to provide for Zion all the essential needs of life in the hardest of times. "The Lord hath chosen Zion; he hath desired it for his habitation. This is my rest for ever: here will I dwell; for I have desired it. I will abundantly bless her provision: I will satisfy her poor with bread. I will also clothe her priests with salvation: and her saints shall shout aloud for joy" (Psalm 132:13-16).

I want to demonstrate to you just how clear and specific God's provision for us will be. The Hebrew word for "provision" in this verse means "lunch, venison, game, supplies, groceries." The Hebrew word for "bread" here means "meat, fruit, bread," as well as "grain for making bread." God is saying, "No matter how difficult your circumstances may look, I'm going to make specific provisions for you. I'll provide you with enough to survive any crisis. You'll be so amazed by it all, you'll shout for joy!"

A young pastor friend of mine in the south told me about a Thanksgiving Day miracle he participated in. He directs an outreach to drug addicts and alcoholics, and he also has a ministry to the poor and needy. During one Thanksgiving holiday, he and a friend distributed turkeys and grocery baskets door to door in a neighborhood known to be the poorest of the poor. When they had only one basket left, they prayed, "Lord, lead us to someone who's been praying for food. We want to see a miracle from you. Show us your divine care for those who trust in you."

With faith that God's Spirit was directing them, they turned down a dirt road and drove along until they came upon a little, run-down shack. They stopped, got out, carried the turkey and grocery basket up to the front door and knocked. From inside they heard a gravelly old man's voice shouting, "Come in!"

The two ministers walked in and saw an elderly man sitting in a wheelchair. He held a Bible in his lap.

My minister friend said to him, "Sir, we're Christians, and we can see you're one too. We don't want to embarrass you in any way, but we believe God has led us here to give you this turkey and these groceries. Would you accept them?"

The man's eyes welled up with tears, and a big smile crossed his face. He yelled into the next room, "I told you, daughter, God would provide our Thanksgiving meal! I told you, I told you. Praise his name!" It turned out the man was a retired preacher and a man of prayer. He testified to my friend that in all his years, God had never failed to provide for him.

God means it when he says, "I will satisfy her poor with food!"

God also promises to preserve Zion in perilous times with creative miracles. Here is one of the most awesome promises in God's word: "When the Lord shall have washed away the filth of the daughters of Zion, and shall have purged the blood of Jerusalem from the midst thereof by the spirit of judgment, and by the spirit of burning. And the Lord will create upon every dwelling place of mount Zion, and upon her assemblies, a cloud and smoke by day, and the shining of a flaming fire by night: for upon all the glory shall be a defense" (Isaiah 4:4-5).

Note the first part of this verse. God makes this promise to a people who've been washed of all their filth, whose sins have been mortified by the judging power of his word and the consuming fire of his Holy Ghost.

You can see this promise isn't for so-called Christians who love Jesus merely in word and not in deed. No, this pledge is effective only for those who are devoted wholly to Christ, who have laid down their evil deeds and are walking in his holiness. The preceding verse claims, "...he that is left in Zion...shall be called holy..." (Isaiah 4:3). Isaiah isn't referring here to a legalistic holiness of the flesh. He's talking about a full surrender to the lordship of Christ, receiving by faith his perfect righteousness and allowing the Holy Ghost to mortify the deeds of the flesh.

God offers this promise to every household in spiritual Zion. He says to his beloved people, "In every dwelling, every family, every congregation – wherever two or three are gathered in my name – I will create a covering of protection, guidance and preservation. The secret behind it all is very simple. Your defense consists of being in my presence. If you live in my presence, you're going to see my creative power manifested in your life."

When hard times come, God will do for us what he's known for: providing deliverance out of nothing. Think about it. When did our Lord ever lose a single creative power? The entire Old Testament cries out to us, "God has always preserved his children creatively and supernaturally!" He created manna in a dry wilderness. He drew forth water from a rock. He closed the mouths of lions and walked through fiery furnaces with his people so they wouldn't be burned. He raised the dead. He supernaturally kept filling a barrel of meal and a bottle of oil so they never went dry. In the New Testament, he turned water into wine, calmed storms, opened prison doors, raised the dead. He did all of these creative miracles for his beloved children of Zion.

My pastor friend Denny Duron testified to me how God brought something out of nothing to preserve his ministry's Christian school in Louisiana. The school had about two thousand children enrolled in a summer program, but it lacked money to provide lunches for them. Denny and his staff began to pray, "Lord, we've got nothing. We need a miracle from you!"

Just when they were on the brink of disaster, their phone rang. It was a trucker, saying, "My vehicle broke down just outside your town. It's loaded with frozen foods, and it's all about to go to waste. I saw your sign, so I thought I'd call to see if you wanted the food. Have you got any freezers?"

Denny was astounded. He said, "Yes, I think we can round up a couple of freezers."

The trucker asked, "A couple? Sir, I don't think you understand. I've got an eighteen-wheeler out here. You're going to need a building full of freezers for all this stuff."

Denny and his staff called around and found some commercial freezer space that was provided free of charge. The frozen food provided those children's lunches.

Beloved, if God has to allow an eighteen-wheeler to break down in front of your house to preserve you, he'll do it. He wants you to know, "I've got a plan of preservation designed especially for you. It's so creative, your mind could never imagine it!"

I'm the first to acknowledge there are a thousand "what if's" to be asked about God's future judgments on the world; but if you're in Zion, none of these things really matter. God is going to receive glory in that evil time through his creative power. He's going to bring out of nothing the full and complete preservation of all who trust him.

The Lord is going to preserve us in Zion because he has set up the throne of Christ there! "Yet have I set my king upon my holy hill of Zion" (Psalm 2:6).

God asks in this psalm, "Why do the heathen rage? Why do they engage in foolish imaginings and counsel? Why do they plot evil against my anointed?" He is aware of all the enemy's attempts to destroy his people. He declares, "Zion will stand! My people will never be vanquished, because I have set my son as king upon my holy hill Zion.

And my son won't relinquish his reign to me '...till he hath put all enemies under his feet'" (1 Corinthians 15:25).

If Christ sits as king and Lord in Zion, then all of his subjects are safe because the ruling potentate has all power to preserve his people. Simply put, as long as Jesus is on his throne, Satan is powerless against us. Of course, you remember where Christ's throne is located. It's in our hearts where he sits ruling and reigning as king and Lord. If we have submitted our hearts and lives to the protecting hands of our king Jesus, then no demonic power or person can pluck us away!

God loves Zion because it is his son's bride, and he's going to act with all his power to preserve this bride. In the Lord's eyes, she is a beautiful joy, and he wants to present her to his son as spotless, pure, full of love and devotion to him. Moreover, this bride represents his promised land. "A land which the Lord thy God careth for: the eyes of the Lord thy God are always upon it, from the beginning of the year even unto the end of the year" (Deuteronomy 11:12). God wants us to know, "My eye is on my people Zion three hundred and sixty-five days a year."

He also gives us these promises about Zion: "I the Lord do keep it; I will water it every moment: lest any hurt it, I will keep it night and day" (Isaiah 27:3). "For the Lord hath chosen Zion; he hath desired it for his habitation" (Psalm 132:13). If the Lord is king in your life, if he has made you his habitation, then who can harm you? Being in Zion means you never have to fear again.

Finally, here is a verse that proves it's impossible for the devil to destroy you because he can't go through the walls God has erected around you: "The oath which he sware to our father Abraham, that he would grant unto us, that we being delivered out of the hand of our enemies might serve him without fear, in holiness and righteousness before him, all the days of our life" (Luke 1:73-75). This deliverance is good for the rest of our lives. We've been set free for the specific purpose of serving our Lord without fear in spite of any storms, holocausts or calamities that come our way.

You don't have to fear a depression, a technological breakdown, or the loss of any provisions or security. God says you are a Zionian, and you've been given ironclad promises that will enable you to live in quiet confidence, no matter what comes.

CHAPTER FIVE

GOD'S CONTROVERSY CONCERNING ZION

"It is the day of the Lord's vengeance, and the year of recompenses for the controversy of Zion."
— Isaiah 34:8.

Isaiah prophesied about a time of retribution that would come upon the nations, and I believe this prophecy includes America. In my opinion, we're now living in the prophetic time Isaiah spoke of, the terrible day of God's recompense. Like other countries around the world, America is facing God's vengeful wrath as payday for offending our holy, compassionate Lord.

Notice in this verse that Isaiah speaks about a "controversy of Zion." What, exactly, does the prophet mean by this? What does it have to do with the judgments gathering over the world? I believe as we examine the judgments taking place all over the earth in each generation, we gain insight into the meaning of Isaiah's prophetic word to us.

As of the late 90s, Russia is falling apart.

Its once-impregnable Iron Curtain has been shredded to pieces. Its government is shaking, and its currency is crashing. Its vital shipyards are shut down. Workers have been unpaid for months, and millions of people have been thrust into poverty.

What does it all mean? Why has God brought such judgment on Russia? In the minds of many Christians, God's controversy with Russia seems obvious. We're seeing the effects of his holy judgment on years of Communism. We think, "God is judging Russia for its barbarianism throughout this century. He's pouring out his wrath on that country because of its wickedness and violence. Russia thumbed its nose at all that's moral and good."

South Korea, Bosnia, Indonesia, Thailand, Japan and the nations of Africa and South America have all been experiencing the day of God's vengeance.

Each of these nations is teetering on the brink of depression, poverty and societal chaos. Much of this calamity is interrelated. Now Indonesia is enduring a 90 percent drop in its real estate and currency, thrusting much of its population into poverty. Some people who were wealthy just a year ago are now living on the streets.

These are just a few examples of how entire nations fall like dominoes. A recent issue of the New York Times quoted the U.S. Secretary of the Treasury as saying, "All nations are being shaken." Little did he know he was quoting the very words of Christ.

Why is all this happening? What is causing God to shake these countries? Is it their suppression of human rights? Is it their idolatry and false religions, their Buddhism, Communism, Hinduism, Islam? What is the wickedness that's bringing down God's sudden wrath on them?

We also have to ask, what is God's controversy with America and these other trembling nations? What's causing the clouds of judgment to gather over the world right now? Isaiah wasn't just making idle talk when he prophesied a great last-days outpouring of God's wrath with recompense and vengeance. By all indications, our nation's time will come one day.

I have no doubt America's judgment will be the most shocking of all because we've sat high and mighty for so long. For generations we've boasted, "We're too big and powerful to fall." Yet this is exactly what Japan's leaders said just eight years before their economy was shattered. They bragged that their country's wealth was so great, the land on which the imperial palace stood was worth more than all the real estate in California combined. As Japan's economy took a drastic nosedive, some of those same financial wizards who spearheaded the nation's prosperity committed suicide.

Is God's controversy with America over its flood of pornography, the thousands upon thousands of internet sites that push filth and smut? Is it the rise of militant homosexuality? Will God destroy us as he did Sodom, for surpassing that society's perversions? Is his controversy over our violence, our rampant immorality or our runaway drug problem as we suck up the majority of the world's illegal supply? Or is his controversy with us over the oceans of innocent blood we've shed by killing millions of unborn children through abortion? What's the controversy that has ignited his wrath toward us?

I have already written about how God will reach the point when he can no longer endure any of these things from us, our violence, bloodshed, degradation, immorality or apostasy. Over the centuries, he has crushed empires whose cups of iniquity overflowed at the very point we have now arrived. Every serious follower of Christ has to realize that America deserves the full fury of God's wrath, but I believe God's controversy with America and the nations goes even beyond depravity and lawlessness.

What is the "controversy of Zion" that Isaiah refers to? First, we need to remember who Zion is. In the previous chapter we noted that all references to Zion in the New Testament point to the overcoming church of Jesus Christ. Now let me offer further proof of this.

There are seven such references to Zion in the New Testament. In one, Paul quotes an Old Testament verse in order to connect Zion to the church of Christ. "As it is written, Behold, I lay in Sion a stumbling stone and rock of offence: and whosoever believeth on him shall not be ashamed" (Romans 9:33).

We know Christ is the foundation stone of spiritual Zion. Paul is proving to us there's a Zion of the New Testament as well as a Zion of the Old. The literal, Old Testament Zion was destroyed, burned to the ground, when the armies of Titus and Cyrus invaded. But God, through his son Jesus Christ, raised up an entirely new holy city, a new Jerusalem coming down out of heaven, populated by a new kind of Jew.

"...There shall come out of Sion the Deliverer, and shall turn away ungodliness from Jacob" (Romans 11:26). "Ye are come unto mount Sion, and unto the city of the living God, the heavenly Jerusalem, and to an innumerable company of angels" (Hebrews 12:22). "Sion" here is identified as a heavenly, spiritual people, a Jerusalem from above made up of spiritual Jews not circumcised physically by the hands of man but circumcised in heart by faith in the son of God. This is a sanctified body of Christ where Jesus is Lord of all.

Indeed, throughout the New Testament, we see that Zion is made up of those who have given themselves wholly to Jesus Christ and who now walk in the power of the Holy Spirit.

So, you ask, what are we to draw from this revelation about Zion? What is Isaiah prophesying about spiritual Zion, the church of Jesus Christ, when he says, "It is the day of the Lord's vengeance...for the controversy of Zion" (Isaiah 34:8)?

Isaiah is saying that right now God has a controversy with all nations, including America, over his church.

We have to understand that all of God's interests in this world are wrapped up in the corporate body of his son, Jesus Christ. Any action he takes on this earth has to do with his concern for his church. Therefore, his controversies with nations go far beyond their immorality, idolatry, sensuality, violence and bloodshed. Every action he takes – whether he prospers a nation or chastens it, blesses it or curses it – is subordinate to his concern for his church.

God has a hidden people in every nation, and his controversies always have to do with his bride in that land. For that reason, I believe that every shaking that's taking place in nations all over the world today – currency problems, economic chaos, bloodshed – has to do with God's controversy over Zion, his body here on earth.

Why did God shake Russia, ripping down its walls and causing its whole interior structure to fall? He was shaking all that stood in the way of his gospel being preached. For decades, he'd watched his spiritual bride in Russia be mocked, hounded, endangered, persecuted. Finally, he said, "Enough! I won't stand by and allow this demonic Iron Curtain to stop my word, my messengers and my missionaries from ministering to my body in this nation."

He humbled the once-powerful bear, all because of his

personal concern for his people there. His judgments on Russia are not about Communism or any other "ism." They are about his controversy over Zion. He's saying to Russia, "Your Communist system is mere dust to me. All I have to do is breathe on it, and in an instant it will blow away. But now you've touched my church, the apple of my eye. You've murdered and sought to destroy my people. Now, Russia, you must face my vengeance. I have a controversy with you because of Zion."

Consider all the terrible stirrings and shakings going on in the Balkans and other Islamic nations. Where have all the ethnic wars and societal turmoil come from? They're the result of God's fury at Islamic fanatics who continue to torture and kill his bride. Many Islamic nations have shut down all Christian missionary work, closing down evangelical churches and persecuting believers. Now God has a controversy with these countries because he has said his gospel will be preached to the ends of the world. I believe he's saying to these nations, "If I have to smite your country and bring it to its knees to open the door to my gospel, I'll do it. My salvation will be preached to all creatures."

Centuries ago, God prospered England, expanding its colonies and territories until they circled the earth. This is where the expression came from, "The sun never sets on the British Empire." Why did God bless England so? What did they do to merit or deserve such favor? God blessed England for the sake of Zion, his church, around the world. He was prospering Great Britain in order to reach the nations of the world with his gospel.

While England was expanding its colonies worldwide, God was raising up powerful preachers in England, Scotland and Wales. His Spirit gave the churches in Britain a heart for world missions. As soon as any British trade ship landed on a colony, a missions outpost quickly sprang up. Every British territory worldwide became a center for spreading the gospel. Great Britain's awesome prosperity was totally subordinate to God's purposes, which were to evangelize unreached nations. It was all for the sake of Zion, even though God later judged England for its merciless methods of colonization.

Sadly, over time England's prosperity brought spiritual decay, lewdness and immorality to the country. The church began to dwindle in numbers and influence, and missionary zeal waned. Eventually, God stripped Britain of its worldwide empire. Hong Kong was the last of its colonial holdouts, and it reverted to Chinese rule in 1997. Why did the British kingdom come down? Was it because the country fell into sensuality and moral decay? That was only part of the reason. It was also because England lost its purpose for being prospered, which was the preservation and blessing of Zion, the bride of Christ.

In 1666, the great city of London was destroyed by fire. The city went up in flames, and many who had become rich through world trade became poor overnight. Multitudes were impoverished.

Some forty-seven years later, while speaking at a commemoration service of the London fire, the pious Puritan John Flavel observed, "London's plague and fire came but three or four years after the casting out and silencing of a great number of able, faithful ministers of Christ there, and all the nation over, because they would not sin against their consciences. Jerusalem was burnt the first time, for misusing the messengers of the Lord (Jeremiah 36:16), and the second time, for laying hands on the disciples of Christ, and persecuting them (Luke 21:12);

for Christ resented what was done against them, as done against himself.

"At least we must be allowed to observe, that the fire happened not six months after the commencing of the Five-Mile Act, by which they who, but a little before, were turned out of their churches, were barbarously turned out of their houses, and not suffered to live within five miles of any corporation, or of the places where they had been ministers. It was the observation of a wise and good man at that time, 'that as it was in mercy to many of the ministers, that they were removed out of the city, before that desolating judgment came; so it spoke aloud to the government, "Let my people go, that they may serve me; and if ye will not, behold, thus and thus will I do unto you."' This he thought was the Lord's voice, then crying in the city."

From 1665 to 1666, London had become a very wicked and godless city. There was much violence, bloodshed and corruption. The state church was mostly backslidden. But God did not send judgment on London until his precious bride was touched by those wicked hands. God's controversy with England had to do with the preservation of Zion.

Likewise, God's initial blessing and prospering of America had a specific purpose. The Lord wanted to raise up a strong church in the United States for the purpose of evangelizing the world, and that's just what happened. Our major universities – Harvard, Yale, Dartmouth, Princeton, Columbia – all began as Bible schools to train pastors and missionaries.

The early American revivals spawned Bible societies, mission societies and great missionary endeavors in all denominations. The common cry of the American church was, "Go into all the world and preach Christ!" At one time, America's most important export was the gospel. Our country sent missionaries all over the world. Eventually, when people in other nations were asked about America, they answered, "That's the missionary country, the gospel people."

I believe this was the reason for God's prospering of our country and this alone. It wasn't because of our ingenuity, our technical skills, our wisdom or our work ethic. No, all our blessings have come because God had his kingdom in mind all along. Everything has been subordinate to his plans for building up his overcoming church.

As happened with Israel, Britain and other highly blessed nations, prosperity ended up deceiving America. Now we've completely forgotten why we were ever blessed. "Jeshurun waxed fat, and kicked: thou art waxen fat, thou art grown thick, thou art covered with fatness; then he forsook God which made him, and lightly esteemed the Rock of his salvation" (Deuteronomy 32:15).

Today, our nation's college campuses are hotbeds of atheism and liberalism. The Bible is rarely mentioned without being mocked or ridiculed. And Americans now spend more on dog food than on missions. Our exports are Coca-Cola, technology, pornography and cults. Years ago, we were seen as a God-blessed land of paradise and refuge for people from all over the world. Now the world sees America as a violent, drug-crazed, money-mad society full of fear and sensuality.

Whenever any nation rises up to seduce or enslave the people of Zion, judgment quickly follows.

Many concerned Christians would say God's controversy is with our political institutions. After all, our governing bodies are constantly making laws that obliterate any semblance of God from our society. They reason it must be the Lord's anger against government leaders and educators who fill the minds of adults and children with anti-God falsehoods.

Of course, God is angry over these things.

Yes, he's going to judge America for such sins, as well as for our violence and bloodshed, our murder of millions of babies, our raging immorality, our sensuality and sexual perversions, our mounting wickedness and debauchery. All of this is so overbearing, it's almost too much to believe. Yet, I tell you, none of these things is God's primary controversy with America.

You might object, "But doesn't the Bible say God destroyed Noah's society with a flood because of his anger over their violence and wicked sins? Didn't the Lord burn down Sodom because he could no longer abide their rampant sexual perversions and acts of violence?"

Yes. In both of these instances, God hated the sins of the wicked. He judges sin no matter who's guilty of it, and regardless of whether it happens in Noah's day, Sodom's day or our day. But there is a more important reason why God had a controversy with those societies, just as he does with ours today. It has to do with the witness of his church.

Let me ask you, how many righteous people do you think were living in Noah's generation when he first began to warn of coming judgment? How many people once gathered with that godly man to believe, share and honor truth? Could it be there were many righteous ones in his society at one point? If so, what happened to them all during the 120 years Noah preached and built the ark so that only Noah and his family were left believing? Were they all seduced into apostasy by the prosperity, materialism and lusts of their day?

I believe God's judgment fell on Noah's society not just because the people rejected his preaching but because Satan had a plan to destroy God's remnant all along. You see, God has a righteous remnant in every generation, and Noah might have been only one of many people in the remnant of his time. Yet, it doesn't matter whether Noah was the only righteous man among his generation or one of many. The point is, God was determined to save his holy seed, the seed whose heel was to crush the serpent's head, by destroying all that could seduce or annihilate it.

In short, Noah represented the only remaining testimony of God, the good news of his salvation to the world; and judgment fell because Satan was out to destroy that testimony. The devil wanted to eliminate the seed of the gospel to save himself, but God acted to eliminate the devil's plan.

Consider also Abraham. You remember that when he prayed over Sodom, he asked God to spare the city if only fifty righteous people remained in it. God promised he would, but then, as Abraham thought about it, he grew a little nervous over how few righteous people might be living in Sodom. So he asked God if he would spare the city for just forty righteous people. Again, God agreed. Abraham kept coming back to him, asking for mercy for fewer numbers until he was down to just ten. Even then, God pledged he would save the entire wicked society of Sodom for the sake of just ten righteous people.

I wonder how many citizens of Sodom had been righteous at one time but were now caught up in that city's flood of iniquity. Could there have been other righteous people with whom Lot found fellowship when he first moved to Sodom? Did Lot tell his uncle Abraham that he felt safe there because he'd found fifty righteous ones like himself? Is that why Abraham felt comfortable asking God for fifty at first?

We do know that, in the end, Lot was the only righteous person living in Sodom. His wife's heart had already been enticed by that wicked society, exposing itself when she turned to look back toward Sodom and was turned into a pillar of salt. We also know Lot's two daughters were immoral. They later got their father drunk for the purpose of having sex with him after Sodom's destruction.

In my mind, this all proves the point I want to make in this chapter. God blesses or disposes of societies and nations according to how they deal with his holy people, Zion, even if Zion consists of only one person.

God will never permit the devil to extinguish his righteous cause nor wipe out his holy witness among a wicked society. He burned Sodom to ashes to prove this to Satan and to all of humankind. He was saying, "No, devil, you're not going to wipe out my remnant. Even if there's just one person remaining who has my testimony, I'll wipe out all your evil to preserve that witness. The gates of hell will not prevail against Zion!"

This principle is clearly illustrated in God's dealing with the heathen nation of Moab. Moab was the nation that hired the prophet Balaam to prophesy against Israel. Of course, God wouldn't allow Balaam to curse Israel, but the prophet did end up counseling Moab to seduce Israel by enticing their men into fornication. Moab's leaders followed his advice by bringing in a religion that involved prostitution. Scripture says Moab "vexed," or troubled, the Israelites with their "wiles," or deceptions (see Numbers 25:17-18).

The Moabites told themselves, "These men of Israel are

sensuous beings. They have a God, but they don't serve him with all their hearts. Even now they're serving false gods. That shows they can be seduced. So, why don't we hold a big feast at the edge of our camp and parade all of these beautiful women in front of them? We can seduce Israel's men with dancing prostitutes. We'll turn them into fornicators!"

Scripture says this is just what happened. "They called the people unto the sacrifices of their gods: and the people did eat, and bowed down to their gods. And Israel joined himself unto Baal-peor: and the anger of the Lord was kindled against Israel" (Numbers 25:2-3).

Up to this time, God did not judge the immorality and idolatry in Moab. He saw that the Moabites were merely doing the deeds of their father, the devil. For years he had left them alone, knowing he would deal with them on judgment day. But now, at the very moment Moab rose up to seduce and deceive his people, God's anger was kindled. He declared, "Moab, I have a controversy with you!"

Of course, God first judged Israel for their sin.

As Peter writes in the New Testament, God's judgment always begins in his own house. Then, scripture says, the Lord declared war on Moab, saying, "Vex the Midianites [Moabites], and smite them: for they vex you with their wiles, wherewith they have beguiled [deceived] you..." (Numbers 25:17-18).

The prophet Jeremiah also spoke against Moab. "Moab shall be destroyed from being a people, because he hath magnified himself against the Lord" (Jeremiah 48:42). "... Moab turned the back with shame! So shall Moab be a derision and a dismaying to all them about him" (Jeremiah 48:39). In similar fashion, Ezekiel, Amos and Zephaniah all prophesied against the Moabites.

Please note, God voiced no controversy with Moab at all until that wicked nation's leaders determined to destroy Israel through lust and deception. Moab had touched the apple of God's eye, and the Lord told them, "I'm going to bring you down from your high place. I'll bring lamentation to all your households, because you've risen up against my holy Zion. I will not allow it."

I hope you can see the parallel with our nation and perhaps understand now why God must judge America. God's controversies with the nations are all about his great love and concern for his church.

The same might be said of America today that was prophesied against Moab. "(You) shall be destroyed from being a people, because he hath magnified himself against the Lord" (Jeremiah 48:42). If it weren't for the church of Jesus Christ in America, God might not have any controversy with our nation as we continue along our sinful path. He would simply deal with our nation on judgment day.

God's beloved bride is part of the populace of this society, however, and she's being threatened by laws that seek to shame and cast out her bridegroom. The Lord's name is being mocked, and his church is being persecuted. Now God is telling America, "I didn't act quickly on my controversy with you about your sensual sins, your debauchery, your pornography, your homosexuality. But now you've touched my church, my body. You've magnified yourself against Zion."

We see a picture of the devil's design against the church in Revelation 12. That chapter tells us Satan is coming down to earth wielding great wrath because he knows his time is short. That's where the devil is right now, not out in the cosmos somewhere but right here in our midst.

He has taken full control of the principalities and powers of darkness, and he's using them all to persecute Zion.

"The serpent cast out of his mouth water as a flood after the woman [the church], that he might cause her to be carried away of the flood...and the dragon was wroth with the woman, and went to make war with the remnant of her seed, which keep the commandments of God, and have the testimony of Jesus Christ" (Revelation 12:15-17).

The woman in this passage is the church, spiritual Zion. After falling to earth, the devil focused on a single goal, to deceive and destroy Zion. Now he has devised a flood of filth, iniquity, deception, false doctrines and false religions with which to try to carry away God's people. He's determined to use this flood to "swallow up" all the citizens of Zion, the bearers of Christ's seal and carriers of his testimony. Right now, we're experiencing the full fury of this demonic flood. In a rush to seem politically correct, politicians and judges and educators are robbing God's people, in league with Satan to extinguish his remnant and testimony.

God is even now acting on his controversy with America, bringing judgment with great anger and vengeance. It's going to happen because Satan has unleashed his flood specifically to destroy not this nation, not wicked sinners, but holy Zion, God's testimony!

At this moment, God still has a strong remnant left in America. He's going to send a message to Satan: "Devil, it's one thing for you to send forth a flood of iniquity and deception to entertain your own people and keep them under your power, but it's another thing for you to direct your flood specifically at my holy Zion. You want to deceive my people to pick them off one by one, attacking the weak, the lame, those who have no vision of Christ.

You want my bride to be a ragged, worn-out, prostituted woman as she approaches marriage with my son. I won't allow it!

"You'll never prevail against my church, devil. I'll bankrupt all of America if I must. I'll ruin your pornographers, your merchandisers, your corrupt, demon-possessed leaders. I'll open up the mouth of the earth and swallow your puny little flood. I'll bring all the help of heaven to aid my holy ones."

We've seen that throughout history God has brought down cities, nations and entire empires just to protect his testimony on earth. God will not hesitate to bring down our country also if it means protecting and preserving his church as a spotless bride for his son, Jesus. I believe that we're going to see God's controversy with America unfold, and it will accomplish two purposes for God: It will smite a nation that has become a willing servant of Satan, and it will purge the church of all hypocrisy.

CHAPTER SIX

PROTECTION IN THE COMING STORM

I've scoured the scriptures, and I can't find a single instance when the Lord judged a people without giving them plenty of warnings in time to repent. Moreover, with every warning God sent, he clearly revealed where people could go to find protection from destruction. Our Lord has always provided refuge for anyone who's willing to honor his word by heeding and obeying it.

In the book of Exodus, God offered his protection to Pharaoh when Moses warned that a great hailstorm was about to strike Egypt. Moses told Pharaoh, "Behold, tomorrow about this time I will cause it to rain a very grievous hail, such as hath not been in Egypt since the foundation thereof even until now" (Exodus 9:18). This warning to Egypt's leaders was a manifestation of God's grace, an offering of love even to wicked Pharaoh and his idolatrous people. God had every right to send that storm upon them without warning because of their continual hardness of heart.

Instead, he told Pharaoh, "I'm going to provide for you, so that you don't have to lose any living thing, including your families, your servants, even your cattle. They all can remain safe. Simply gather up everyone and everything and flee into your houses. Get under a roof somewhere and take cover, and you'll be safe from the storm."

All these people had to do to be safe was to honor the Lord's word to them, to believe that a storm was coming. As it turned out, many did fear the Lord, acknowledging his word by fleeing to their houses. "He that feared the word of the Lord among the servants of Pharaoh made his servants and his cattle flee into the houses: and he that regarded not the word of the Lord left his servants and his cattle in the field…and the hail smote throughout all the land of Egypt all that was in the field, both man and beast…" (Exodus 9:20-21, 25).

Tragically, everyone who didn't heed the warning lost everything that was not under cover, but those who believed God's warnings were protected. After the storm was over, they came out of their homes and saw they still had their cattle and servants. Everything had remained safe under the roof of the house, just as the Lord had said. They'd received his protection from the storm just by obeying his word.

I want to show you from the scriptures that God has made us the very same promise today.

Does God keep his word, or are his warnings in vain? Will he send forth his prophets and watchmen with warnings but then do nothing?

Whenever a people in history have hardened their hearts, God has given them over to what's called a "judicial blindness." This judgment falls upon all those who mock the word of God. It causes them to claim a false security and to trust in lies, all in an effort to preserve their greedy dreams. It distorts their thinking and planning, and it dulls their ears to every warning of reality.

Hardhearted people can look straight into the face of a coming storm and see only a gentle breeze.

I believe our President, Congress and politicians are under just such a judicial blindness from God, except for a few believers among them who fear and honor his word. One Christian senator has admitted, "Washington is blind to what's happening in the world and to our economy." He's right. Just one small, technical problem could blow away our prosperity in an instant.

I've read a news report that deeply disturbs me. A study by a national team of psychologists revealed that many Americans are experiencing what's called "psychological denial." The study says people are unwilling to believe that any loss – financial or otherwise – could happen to them. It's a recipe for total disaster. If people don't believe chaos can befall them, how will they ever listen to warnings about the storm that's racing toward us?

The prophet Isaiah speaks of a people who were just like this. They were full of pride, flaunting an insolent self-confidence. They felt they didn't have to account for their lives, so they no longer feared God, hell or even death. They all reasoned they had accumulated enough money, gathered enough resources and made enough covenants with surrounding countries to be totally protected from any disaster. They thought they'd built for themselves a special hiding place where no storm could reach them.

Isaiah responded to their arrogance with these shocking words: "Wherefore hear the word of the Lord, ye scornful men, that rule this people which is in Jerusalem. Because ye have said, We have made a covenant with death, and with hell are we at agreement; when the overflowing scourge shall pass through, it shall not come unto us: for we have made lies our refuge, and under falsehood have we hid ourselves" (Isaiah 28:14-15).

What an amazing word. It perfectly describes our nation today. There is no fear of God in the land anymore, no fear of hell, of judgment, of having to stand before God and account for one's life. It's true that some nonbelievers are expecting a storm to come; but instead of turning to the Lord, they're building up their own secret stash of money. Proud and arrogant, they think, "I can ride out any storm. I've made my fortune. I've built a place to hide up in my mountain retreat. When all the cities start to go up in flames, I'll be living a king's life away from it all. No storm can ever reach me."

Such was the thinking in Israel, but Isaiah warned that God was about to send a storm so powerful that it would wipe out all such arrogance. "...the hail shall sweep away the refuge of lies, and the waters shall overflow the hiding place. And your covenant with death shall be disannulled, and your agreement with hell shall not stand; when the overflowing scourge shall pass through, then ye shall be trodden down by it" (Isaiah 28:17-18). Isaiah was telling Israel, "All of you who agreed there was no death, no hell, no judgment. You're going to be trodden down by the Lord's raging storm. You won't be able to find safety from it anywhere. There is no hiding place for the proud and unbelieving."

Isaiah warned, "Now therefore be ye not mockers, lest your bands be made strong: for I have heard from the Lord God of hosts a consumption, even determined upon the whole earth" (Isaiah 28:22). The prophet was saying: "You may think you have a hiding place, but it's a false security! Your man-made refuge is going to fail, because God's storm is going to smash it into pieces. Everything you have is going to come down, and you'll be terrified when you realize what's happening. By then it will be too late for you."

Suddenly, the Holy Ghost stopped Isaiah in the very midst of his message of judgment. The Spirit of God stopped the prophet from speaking, as if to say, "Wait, Isaiah. I don't want you to speak another word of judgment until my people know what I'm going to do for them."

Then God gave Isaiah a message of hope. He instructed the prophet to deliver it to everyone who believed on the Lord and trusted in his word. "Therefore thus saith the Lord God, Behold, I lay in Zion for a foundation a stone, a tried stone, a precious corner stone, a sure foundation: he that believeth shall not make haste" (Isaiah 28:16). The message was, "Anyone who believes on this stone will not be disturbed."

We know that the stone Isaiah is talking about is Jesus Christ, our savior and Lord. We're to believe on him for all things; he alone is to be the solid rock on which we stand. As the Old Testament tells us, "Their rock is not as our Rock..." (Deuteronomy 32:31). This means that as followers of Jesus, we're not to put our trust in the things the world trusts in.

For example, even though Social Security may never fail, we're not to put our trust in it for our future provision. That isn't a sure foundation, nor can we put our trust in retirement funds even if they endure the storm. These are not a solid, tried stone. Our only secret hiding place is in Christ. If we're standing on him, the Rock, we can't be disturbed, no matter what terrible news may come.

The storms ahead may be so severe that they could bring chaos to the whole world, and out of that chaos could emerge the beast and the Antichrist. Therefore, we can't afford to trust technology, education, science, medicine or even our mighty armed forces to rescue us. Ultimately, these are all failing foundations. The apostle Paul echoes Moses in 1 Corinthians 10:4, saying our Rock is Christ. The psalmist concurs, "The Lord is my rock, and my fortress, and my deliverer..." (Psalm 18:2). "For in the time of trouble he shall hide me in his pavilion: in the secret of his tabernacle shall he hide me; he shall set me up on a rock" (Psalm 27:5). Our only safe ground, our only solid Rock is Jesus himself!

David speaks in Psalm 31 of a "house of defense," a secret hiding place in God's presence. David cried out to God, "...be thou my strong rock, for an house of defense to save me" (Psalm 31:2). I mentioned at the beginning of this chapter that God warned Egypt, "If you want to be protected from the storm, flee to your house." Now we see in David's prayer a strikingly similar image. He's calling on God to be a place of refuge.

Where is this "house of defense" David refers to? Where is the place of protection God has provided for his people today?

I don't believe it's some place we can physically find and hide in. It's not in some remote hiding place. No, David is speaking here of the secret place of prayer. The only way we can get to that safe place is on our knees.

God's word tells us again and again that the only safe hiding place in the storm is any room or space where we can go to seek the face of the Lord. The prophet Elijah knew this. That's why he shut himself in when he was called upon to pray over a dead child. Scripture says, "He went in therefore, and shut the door upon them twain, and prayed unto the Lord" (2 Kings 4:33). Elijah knew the only way through a hopeless, lifeless situation was to go into a room, shut the door and get hold of God.

This is the same lesson every Christian in America needs to learn: Our place of safety is our secret closet of prayer.

When the storm hits, we won't be able to sit about idly, saying, "Sure, I believe the Lord. I trust in him." We're going to have to act on that trust! We're told to "flee to our house," to go to our secret chamber and seek God diligently. Jesus instructed, "Watch ye and pray, lest ye enter into temptation" (Mark 14:38). He was saying, in other words, "Spend your energies seeking me, so you won't be tempted to fret, worry or doubt in the midst of the storm."

You don't need to turn to anyone for advice. You need only to run to your secret closet of prayer where your father awaits you. You see, that secret room is your place of counsel as well as your place of safety. In Psalm 102, God assures us of his presence in our times of worry and fear. This psalm is even titled "A Prayer of the afflicted, when he is overwhelmed, and poureth out his complaint before the Lord." Verse 17 promises, "He will regard the prayer of the destitute, and not despise their prayer."

Yet, be warned. When you go into your secret closet and shut the door behind you, be very careful how you pray. There is a certain kind of praying that God will accept from sinners but not from his children. This kind of praying truly displeases him. The psalmist gives us evidence of this, writing, "O Lord God of hosts, how long wilt thou be angry against the prayer of thy people?" (Psalm 80:4).

God is displeased with those who pray with a despondent, defeatist attitude.

Why? He doesn't want his children to come into his

presence groveling like beggars! As I spent time in prayer recently, the Lord convicted me about this very issue. For several days, I had offered up prayers to him with what I thought were godly tears, yet God showed me my prayers were utterly unworthy of his name and power. You may ask, "Doesn't God care about all the prayers of his children? Doesn't he promise to hear our cry, no matter what our state may be?"

Not necessarily. Here is how I was praying: "Lord, why am I not receiving the revelation of you that I so hunger and thirst for? I don't seem to be growing in the knowledge of you as I should. My spiritual eyes see so little, my ears seem so dull, and my heart feels so thick. Father, I've been serving you all these years, but I feel inadequate, spiritually ignorant, far behind in knowing your ways as I ought. Please, show me if there's anything hindering me from receiving your revelation. Is there a sin in my heart I'm not aware of? What's keeping me from growing in the deeper things of your kingdom?"

I prayed on and on this way until suddenly the Holy Ghost stopped me. God picked me up from the floor, stood me on my feet, and spoke powerfully to me in that still, small voice I know is his. "David, stop sniveling in my presence. Your praying this way brings me no pleasure. You're totally forgetting all the things I've done for you these past years. You don't realize it, but when you tell me your eyes are dim, your ears are dull and your heart is thick, you're not expressing true humility. On the contrary, you're discrediting all my good work in you.

"You're saying I've ignored all your prayers, that my Spirit in you has simply stood by, never anointing my word in you. You're telling me that all of the word you've heard and preached throughout the years has gone straight through you, without ever changing you. You're saying that in the face of all your sincere crying to me – all your hungering and thirsting, all your readiness to hear and obey – you've been left a stunted, ignorant, blind, spiritual idiot.

"You're discrediting everything I've done in you, and I won't accept it. You're overlooking all your growth. You're blinding yourself to all the changes I've made in you as well as all the wonderful things I've done through you. In Christ you're not blind, deaf and dumb. Rather, you are and have been changing from glory to glory. David, you should be coming to me with thanksgiving for all I've done!"

How must the Lord feel when we beg him to supply all of our future needs, and yet we discredit what he has already done for us in the past?

How it must grieve God when we don't acknowledge his past work in us, when we don't thank him for all the storms he's brought us through and the victories he's given us. If we're going to be kept safe in the coming storm, then we must come to God with thanksgiving today, saying, "Lord, you've kept me all these years. If you can deliver me from all my sins, I know you can take care of all my physical needs."

Are you thankful to the Lord for all the things he's done in your life? Or do you forget them all in your times of trouble?

As you come to the Lord in prayer, don't focus on all that has yet to be done in you. Don't complain about all your weaknesses and shortcomings. Instead, thank him, saying, "Father, I'm grateful for your Holy Ghost in me, for changing me, for opening your word to me, for giving me the desire to obey you. Thank you for all your blessings up to now!"

Even if someday our national government fails – even if our major cities are set aflame and martial law is declared – God's people will still have nothing to fear. If we're going to trust our father to keep us through every grievous storm, then we need to start thanking him now for delivering us from all storms in the past. We have to stop groveling like beggars before him. Instead, we should pray, "Yes, Lord. I'll pray diligently through the storm. I know you'll hear my prayers. You'll provide for my family. You'll be faithful to keep us from hunger and homelessness. You're going to prepare a table for us in the time of famine and terror."

CHAPTER SEVEN

ARMAGEDDON AND THE MARK OF THE BEAST

It's a simple fact of human nature that the more perilous the times become the more people become inter-
ested in prophesied future events. Even the secular
world is becoming preoccupied with biblical warnings
about cataclysmic events in the future. In the summer of
1998, Hollywood made millions of dollars on films such as
Armageddon, Deep Impact and others featuring end-time
subjects. At any given moment, printing presses around
the world churn out a myriad of books on prophetic subjects, such as the Antichrist, the battle of Armageddon,
the mark of the beast, and the prophecies of Daniel and
the book of Revelation.

I finally decided I would try to find out what the prophecy "experts" were saying. I asked my secretary to go
to a Christian bookstore near our offices and pick out
any titles that have been written on these subjects. She
brought back a tall stack of newly released books. The
title of one volume, by a British writer, was The Antichrist and a Cup of Tea. In the book, the author suggests
England's Prince Charles may be a part of the Antichrist
system because his coat of arms bears a depiction of

what the author calls "the first beast." This clue, he says, tells us the mark of the beast may be initiated by Prince Charles's bank in England.

As I glanced through the rest of the books, I realized that few agreed about the apocalyptic events foretold in scripture. Some took a pre-tribulation view of Christ's return, meaning they believe the rapture of all believers will occur before the seven-year period of worldwide woes begins. (This period of tribulation is also known as "Jacob's troubles.") Several other writers take a mid-tribulation view, claiming the rapture will occur after three-and-a-half years of troubles, midway through the great tribulation. Still others take a post-tribulation stance, believing Christians will endure the entire seven-year period of worldwide tribulation.

No matter what your view is, you probably swallow hard when you hear warnings that believers are going to suffer hard times as end-time events draw closer. Of course, no one wants to hear this kind of news. In fact, numbers of people have written to our ministry demanding to know where I stand on these prophetic issues. Some have implied they would no longer read or listen to any of my messages unless I preach a pre-tribulation escape from all the troubles that are coming.

Here is my view on these subjects: I believe Jesus can return at any moment. Christ himself says he will come in the twinkling of an eye and at a time when we least expect him. Therefore, I believe it is dangerous and even evil to suggest that "the Lord delays his coming." Jesus' parable on the evil servant states this clearly enough. Scripture makes it crystal clear we are to be prepared for his return at all times, to remain awake, expectant and "dressed to meet him." For this reason, I believe no

Christian who is a true overcomer will be caught unaware because he'll continually be looking for his bridegroom to come for him.

Having said this, I also believe Christians are going to endure a great measure of suffering. Already many devoted believers worldwide are undergoing intense persecution. For example, if you were to talk to Christians living in Indonesia today, they might tell you they're in the midst of the great tribulation. Hundreds of Chinese Christians in that country were slain in riots by Muslim mobs. Their businesses were burned to the ground, and numbers of believers were jailed. These Christians are fully aware they are being pursued and persecuted by demonic forces. When they gather together, their cry is "Even so, come quickly, Lord Jesus!"

At Times Square Church, we count among our congregation many young career people from various nations. Some of these young men and women don't even know if their families are still alive in their homeland. Our office regularly receives news reports from missions agencies that cover persecution of the church around the world. Persecution continues all over the globe.

Believers in nations throughout Asia and Africa, especially, are being murdered, mutilated, ostracized, cut off from their families, their children taken from them. They're enduring tribal uprisings, racial wars, machete-wielding rebel fanatics. Thousands have had to flee their homes and villages, and they've ended up in refugee camps. Even professionals have been fired from their jobs and driven from their communities.

If you were to preach to these believers, "All Christians are going to be delivered before the tribulation comes," they wouldn't feel compelled to believe you. After all, they haven't been rescued from their present sufferings. They would tell you, "We are in the tribulation."

There are multitudes of such godly saints around the world to whom the Antichrist, Armageddon and the mark of the beast have no meaning whatsoever. We in America have the luxury of studying and speculating on these prophetic events, even flocking to prophecy conferences by the thousands while our brothers and sisters in other nations have to pay for their faith with their lives. I know of many of these Christians in other lands who believe the antichrist spirit is now in full control, and they're resisting him to the point of shedding blood.

Any talk of a future war such as Armageddon doesn't concern them because they're already in a battle just to survive each day.

My point here isn't to ridicule prophecy specialists or Christians who attend prophecy conferences. Rather, it is to convince you we dare not overlook the fact that many of our Christian brothers and sisters are right now suffering through incredible hardships and persecution. Also, I believe it grieves the Lord to see Christians looking so intensely into the future and neglecting the present apathy of their own hearts. Simply put, there is too much confusing talk in the church right now about subjects such as the Antichrist, Armageddon and the mark of the beast.

Many Christians are talking now more than ever about the coming of the devil as the incarnate "man of sin" or Antichrist. Like the vast majority of evangelical Christians, I believe a devil-possessed monarch will rise up in God's appointed time, but a future Antichrist is of no concern to me, nor should he be to any of God's people.

I have no doubt whatsoever that when the man of sin

comes to power, every overcoming believer will already be with Jesus. The very thought that Christ would allow a devil-incarnated czar to seduce his beloved bride into worshiping a beast is beyond my comprehension. I simply can't accept the idea that our Lord would stand by and allow the devil to molest his son's own bride just prior to the wedding feast. That's impossible. Christ's bride will not be raped by the devil's Antichrist in her last hour.

I believe the more important matter to understand right now is that an antichrist spirit has been at work in the world since the cross. "Little children, it is the last time: and as ye have heard that antichrist shall come, even now are there many antichrists; whereby we know that it is the last time" (1 John 2:18). John tells us plainly here that we're to beware of the spirit of antichrist warring against us in the present. He's not talking only about some future superman but an antichrist spirit that's at work right now, attempting to deceive the elect.

"Many deceivers are entered into the world, who confess not that Jesus Christ is come in the flesh. This is a deceiver and an antichrist" (2 John 1:7).

"Who is a liar but he that denieth that Jesus is the Christ? He is antichrist, that denieth the Father and the Son" (1 John 2:22).

"Every spirit that confesseth not that Jesus Christ is come in the flesh is not of God: and this is that spirit of antichrist, whereof ye have heard that it should come; and even now already is it in the world" (1 John 4:3).

In short, John is saying, "Anyone who denies that Jesus is God in flesh has the spirit of antichrist." He's warning us to watch out for religious people who would rob us of our faith in Christ as the divine son of the living God. By John's definition, this would include many church leaders today. For example, a survey revealed that less than forty percent of ministers in a certain liberal, Protestant organization believe in the virgin birth. They reject Jesus as the Christ, that is, as God come in the flesh.

You can talk convincingly about a man of sin who will come to deceive the nations. The fact is his spirit is already at work in the world. John says, "You've heard about a coming Antichrist. Well, he's already here, and he's at work in corrupt, blaspheming ministers."

The antichrist spirit isn't something you discern in a homosexual hangout or a barroom full of alcoholics or in our halls of education or government.

No, John says you find it in the backslidden, sin-condoning, perversion-excusing, lust-laden church and its faithless preachers and teachers.

Is the world going to see a literal war called Armageddon, which will be fought in the Middle East? I believe there will be a gathering of nations for the battle of Armageddon, just as the Bible predicts.

"I saw three unclean spirits like frogs come out of the mouth of the dragon, and out of the mouth of the beast, and out of the mouth of the false prophet. For they are the spirits of devils, working miracles, which go forth unto the kings of the earth and of the whole world, to gather them to the battle of that great day of God Almighty. Behold, I come as a thief. Blessed is he that watcheth, and keepeth his garments, lest he walk naked, and they see his shame. And he gathered them together into a place called in the Hebrew tongue Armageddon" (Revelation 16:13-16).

Like the Antichrist, this last great battle between God and the nations should not be our main concern. All the wicked, rebellious nations involved are going to be swept away like dust by a single word from God's mouth. "Behold, the nations are as a drop of a bucket, and are counted as the small dust of the balance: behold, he taketh up the isles as a very little thing" (Isaiah 40:15). "All nations before him are as nothing; and they are counted to him less than nothing, and vanity" (Isaiah 40:17).

Why should I concern myself about "gathering nations" and Armageddon when my God says they're nothing in his sight? He's going to blow away every power in an instant with a mere breath from his mouth.

The war we need to focus on right now is the one that's taking place in our hearts. Puritan theologians depicted Armageddon as a symbolic battle, one that's being waged for the soul of the bride of Christ. It's a battle that began at Calvary and will end only with the second coming of our Lord. Our battle isn't with the beast of John's revelation, but with the beast within us. Satan is waging war on Christ's bride, attempting to turn her into a doubting, dysfunctional harlot before her wedding day. Therefore, all our war efforts should be concentrated on these daily battles, not on some strategy against a man of sin who's still to come.

Tragically, multitudes of Christians within the past two thousand years have done a lot of thinking and teaching about the great battle of Armageddon only to lose the daily battle with sin. Such people were consumed with figuring out prophecies, yet many ended up lost because they ignored the battle that took place in their own hearts.

What good is it to accumulate an entire storehouse of prophetic knowledge, preaching and teaching it in detail, if you drift away from intimacy with Christ? You can know everything possible about all these prophetic subjects and yet still fall into the jaws of lust, lose your faith and die in utter apathy.

Peter warns us, "Dearly beloved, I beseech you as strangers and pilgrims, abstain from fleshly lusts, which war against the soul" (1 Peter 2:11). He's saying, "You've got to face a battle every day, and it's a battle with lust. Armageddon? You've got Armageddon in your soul! You have to focus on that as your main battle."

The mark of the beast is a prophetic event that has brought much fear and confusion to the body of Christ. The church is being inundated right now with ingenious but very confusing explanations about the meaning of the mark of the beast.

It is true the Bible speaks very clearly of a time coming when no one will be able to buy or sell if they don't bear the mark, and no one can get the mark without worshiping the beast. What a horrible time that's going to be. Without this mark there will be no way to obtain food or transportation or even to make a living. It will be humanly impossible to survive. The mere thought of such a scenario is frightening to many Christians as they contemplate ending up poverty-stricken vagabonds, living on handouts and miracles.

Such fear is unfounded, though, for true believers.

The technology is already in place to implement just such a "marking" system. Bio-chip implants, each the size of a grain of rice, can be tucked under a person's skin to monitor all his buying and selling transactions. Other similar high-tech identification systems have been developed as well: eye scans, facial scans, palm printing, transponders. But, at this point, I'll leave all speculation about the beast's marking system to the writers on prophecy who are preoccupied with its technology.

Some pre-tribulation teachers say that after Christ takes away his church, those who are left behind may be saved only if they refuse the mark of the beast. Revelation warns, "...If any man worship the beast and his image, and receive his mark in his forehead, or in his hand, the same shall drink of the wine of the wrath of God..." (Revelation 14:9-10). Some present-day authors have written books for those left behind, urging them not to accept the mark. They suggest their only hope lies in this verse: "...them that had gotten the victory over the beast, and over his image, and over his mark, and over the number of his name, stand on the sea of glass, having the harps of God" (Revelation 15:2). My belief is that the overcoming church of Jesus Christ will be with the Lord when this marking takes place.

God's people have already been marked on their foreheads. Ezekiel spoke of a people "...that sigh and that cry for all the abominations that be done in the midst..." (Ezekiel 9:4). In Revelation 7:3, we hear the Lord telling the destroying angels, "Hurt not the earth, neither the sea, nor the trees, till we have sealed the servants of our God in their foreheads." In Revelation 9:4 the demon powers unleashed in the last days are commanded not to touch "...those men which have...the seal of God in their foreheads." Best of all, in Revelation 22:4 we have the promise, "They shall see his face; and his name shall be in their foreheads."

We, his children, are already marked in our foreheads. We are blood-purchased, sealed, marked and preserved for glory. Who dares try to convince us that he who sealed us in our foreheads would allow Satan to replace the Lord's mark with his own? I have no room on my forehead for the devil's mark. My forehead has already been claimed, and my forearm has been plunged beneath the blood of God's lamb. The mark of the beast has nothing to do with the true believer.

Also, in my opinion, it is unbecoming of Christians – and a poor testimony to the world – to be combative over whether overcoming believers will be taken before, during or after the tribulation. There are godly people who argue for every theological side, and each group has scriptures in abundance to back up its position.

To me, none of this really matters. What is truly important is, no matter what comes, the Bible gives us covenant promises that God will never leave us orphaned. He will walk with us through fire, flood or famine. He will sustain us in the midst of depression and disaster. If he can empower the Hebrew children to go through the fiery furnace and Daniel to endure the lions' den, then he can empower us all to resist anything the devil throws at us. We're his bride, and his love will deliver us.

I personally believe God is going to remove his bride before he pours out his final vials of wrath upon the earth. Yes, I look continually for Jesus' coming.

While so many Christians are focusing on Armageddon, a more important prophetic event is taking place; and most Christians seem not to be aware of it.

Without question, the Lord will bring judgment upon some nations for their vicious attacks on God's children. The Lord is clearly saying to them, "I have a controversy with any nation that touches my bride." God obviously has a controversy with America also. Our political leaders, judges and educators have made it "politically correct," even chic, to harass the body of Christ. Our laws and statutes have already removed the ten commandments from our halls of justice, and now they're set upon removing God's name from our coins. The government allows schools to pass out condoms to children, yet they ban prayer and God's name from the classroom.

I believe all of these things — the exaltation of depravity, as well as the push to destroy everything holy in our society — are some of the reasons America will come under God's chastening. Yet there is an even more exact cause behind all of God's awesome shakings throughout the world.

Christ is taking his chosen people into a wilderness as an opportunity to find a remnant who will fully trust him as savior and provider.

God's word contains a glorious promise that remains yet unclaimed by his people. It is a promise meant especially for times like these. It is God's promise of rest to his people. "There remaineth therefore a rest to the people of God" (Hebrews 4:9).

Even in King David's day, God was still looking for a people who would enter into this divine rest. Up to that time, only a few of his children had known his rest. Tragically, God's rest remains largely unclaimed by his people today. This is why the author of Hebrews urges us, "Let us labour therefore to enter into that rest, lest any man fall after the same example of unbelief" (Hebrews 4:11). Rest is total trust in God for all things.

When God took Israel into the wilderness, he did it for the specific purpose of bringing them into his rest. He stripped the people of all their human resources, removing from them all visible means of support. They had no food, no water, no houses, no employment, no source for any necessity other than the Lord himself. God was asking them to live by faith alone in him as their security and source for all things. He told them, "I will be your God, your everything. Simply believe and trust in me."

Despite this, they failed miserably. They saw the Lord provide miracle after miracle of deliverance on their behalf. They saw him provide bread from heaven, meat from the sky, water from a rock. Still they murmured and complained about their life in the wilderness. They even accused the Lord of trying to kill them by taking away all their means of survival.

What horrible unbelief! God grieved over these ungrateful, untrusting people for forty years. Yet I believe God has an even greater grief over his church today. I ask you, as he beholds his children right now, what does he see?

He sees a people who fret and worry about maintaining their lifestyle. Many believers today have grown indifferent and apathetic to the things of God. Instead, they've become wrapped up in worldly activities and material pursuits. They have no time to seek him with their whole heart. Some even pray for revival selfishly, wanting God to be appeased so he won't take away their prosperity.

He sees his children worrying about Social Security, retirement funds, mortgage payments, investments. He sees them full of anxiety and fear as if their survival depends on their ingenuity and wisdom or upon the good faith of the government.

One day, God will take his church into a wilderness of testing to strip away our human reserves and make us wholly dependent on him.

Our Lord will take away our ease, our great financial flow, our high-tech resources we thought would always be available. Why? He's doing it because our present generation has never had to trust him, whether for food, shelter, jobs or daily supplies. We've grown lukewarm, self-reliant, enticed by material things. Eventually, we may be thrust into a different kind of world altogether, a world of vanishing employment, scarcity, physical deprivation, many sellers and few buyers. It will happen as God's way of wooing us back to himself. He's going to awaken us to our need for faith and bring us into his rest, and he's going to do it all out of love.

God foretells all of this through the prophet Hosea. "Therefore will I return, and take away my corn in the time thereof, and my wine in the season thereof, and will recover my wool and my flax given to cover her nakedness. And now will I discover her lewdness in the sight of her lovers, and none shall deliver her out of mine hand. I will also cause all her mirth to cease, her feast days, her new moons, and her sabbaths, and all her solemn feasts. And I will destroy her vines and her fig trees, whereof she hath said, These are my rewards that my lovers have given me: and I will make them a forest, and the beasts of the field shall eat them" (Hosea 2:9-12).

The Lord is warning us in this passage, "The party's over, folks. All the drunkenness, all the gloating over possessions and abundance, it's ending, right now. All these things people trusted in — wealth, jewels, riches — are about to turn to dust before your eyes."

CHAPTER EIGHT

CRAVING THE PRESENCE OF THE LORD

Whenever people ask me about what's going to happen to America's economy, I give them the truth, but they quickly want to change the subject. Everyone senses that something is about to take place, but no one wants to face it. A lawyer friend of mine had the typical response. He said, "I know something unusual is happening and that a storm is probably coming. But I really don't want to hear about it. I just hope it blows over, and everything gets back to normal as quickly as possible."

Others take my warnings lightly, as if they're part of some personal theory or even a doctrinal aberration. They simply don't want to hear any bad news. You also may be weary of hearing about the coming storm, and you may want to shut it out of your mind, but that won't change the reality of what's already happening on a global scale.

On the day the U.S. stock market crashed in 1929, ushering in the Great Depression, Elliott Bell of the New York Times described the atmosphere on Wall Street, "It was the most terrifying and unreal day I have ever seen on Wall Street. It began on a cool and overcast day. A light, northeast wind blew down the canyons of Wall Street. The temperature was in the fifties, and bankers and brokers buttoned their topcoats.

"About eleven o'clock, the storm broke. It was a deluge. It came with a ferocity that left men dazed. The bottom simply fell out of the market. Wall Street became a nightmarish spectacle. Traders who a few short days before had visions of wealth saw all their hopes smashed in a collapse so devastating, so far beyond their wildest fears, as to seem unreal. The storm created a sense of danger like that which grips men on a sinking ship."

This chapter concerns the spiritual condition of God's people and how they react in perilous times. I believe our Lord is concerned about how we'll react when we begin to witness all the disasters that soon will hit our nation. He knows our lifestyle is going to change in ways we could never imagine, and he wants us to be prepared.

Even now, I realize that every foolish, frivolous thing in my life must go. Every ungodly ambition, covetous desire, selfish dream, root of bitterness, worldly attachment – everything that has corrupted or hindered my communion with the Lord – has to change. Life should not go on as usual for any of us. If we are to endure, our walk with the Lord must be vastly different from the way it is today.

The overwhelming majority of Americans, including multitudes of Christians, have been consumed with fascination over the sexual sin and debauchery with our politicians. This fascination is simply incomprehensible to the rest of the world, especially as it crumbles into economic ruin. The international ridicule being heaped on us is all part of God's judgment on our country. He has made America the laughingstock of the world, shaming and humbling us in the eyes of other nations.

God is shaking everything that can be shaken in nations all over the world. Bankruptcies and unemployment are causing suicides. The United States, the world's great superpower, will one day see its economy smashed. Americans are going to have to face conditions of scarcity and privation. I wonder what will be most important to us in the midst of the storm?

We certainly won't be thinking about whether we're fulfilled by our jobs, whether we're getting good counseling or whether we have the best home or car our finances will allow. Instead, everything at that time will boil down to some very basic questions. I believe our task right now is to find out what those important issues will be.

I think I found my answer during a recent trip my wife and I took to Israel. The discovery came to me while I was praying on Mount Carmel. I asked my host to drop me off at a private area near the top of the mountain. I wanted to spend a few hours soaking in a sense of the place, to see if the Lord had anything special to say to me while I spent time alone with him.

As soon as I got out of the car, I found myself looking down over the valley leading to Jezreel. It was an amazing sight. I pictured the prophet Elijah outrunning King Ahab's chariot across the plain. Today, it takes a car half an hour to drive that distance, some twenty-six miles. What supernatural power it took for Elijah to perform such a feat.

I thought, "It was somewhere near this very spot that Elijah built an altar and called down fire out of heaven. Four hundred false prophets were slain on that day. The very ground I'm standing on soaked up their blood."

I turned to my left and saw the blue Mediterranean. "It was here that Elijah prayed seven times for rain. The small cloud he saw — the one the size of a man's fist — must have come from that direction, which is now the port of Haifa."

As I looked down the mountainside of Carmel, I wondered, "How did Elijah get all those barrels of water up here, especially during a famine? It seems so unreal how these things could have happened. Yet we know they're true. The Lord did them all for his people."

I waited there on the mount, hoping I might be struck by some special feeling or revelation from the Lord. And I began to pray: "Lord, I'm standing where Elijah stood. And I'm praying where he prayed. Your word says Elijah was a man subject to human passions just like us. That means I can pray and reach you, just as he did. Speak to me, father. Please let me hear what you want to say to my spirit."

No special release ever came to me. Perhaps that had to do with the sight of all the empty, crumpled Coke cans and McDonald's burger wrappers cluttering the bushes around the area. Maybe it was the teenagers talking casually and making out in a car nearby. In any case, I received nothing from the Lord that day.

Later, I felt the same disappointment at Christ's tomb in Jerusalem and at the other so-called sacred sites. Even the garden of Gethsemane did nothing for me. Perhaps it was because of all the crass commercialism surrounding these special places. Nothing at all hit me from the Lord.

The main reason we had traveled to Israel was to dedicate a new church our ministry helped to build on Mount Carmel. That was a wonderful experience. To see the glory of the Lord and the holy fire of God's Spirit fall from heaven during the dedication service was awesome. Between our meetings and travels, I carved out quality time to be alone with the Lord in prayer. I was grateful to have that precious time with him.

Yet I felt a growing sense in my soul that something was missing on our mission. I knew we were in God's perfect will by being there; after all, we were sent there by his clear direction. Despite that, our trip just didn't provide the sense of fulfillment I thought it should. Something kept gnawing at my spirit about the matter.

I didn't recognize what that missing element was until we were on the way home, airborne some thirty thousand feet over the Atlantic. That's when it struck me: I was heading home, only my sense of "home" wasn't about a house or apartment. Rather, it was that soon I would be within our house, in a particular room, a place I think of as my "craving room."

The word "crave" means "long for, eagerly desire, yearn deeply, go after, pursue, lay hold of." The room I'm talking about is more than just a prayer room for me. It's where I go to meet with my beloved Lord to spill to him the very longings of my soul. It's where I long after him freely and have face-to-face communion with him. I realized on that plane flight that I have a constant craving to go to that room. This craving grows stronger and stronger within me every day.

I realized too that Mount Carmel was Elijah's "craving place." He went there many times to pray, and Jesus went often to the mountains to pray. That was his special place to commune with the father. Every prophet in the Bible had a special "craving place." I believe every Christian who's serious about his walk with the Lord should have one too.

When we finally got home from our trip, I went into my craving room the first chance I got. I shut the door, raised my hands to heaven and began to cry, "Oh, Lord, I missed you! I've missed this secret place where we meet. I've been yearning for a week to get back to this trysting spot with you. This is my garden of Gethsemane, my Mount Carmel, the place where I come to commune with you."

It was in my "craving" room that God spoke to me.

I am fully convinced God is going to miraculously protect and provide for his people in the most difficult times ahead. Our Lord will not abandon his own children in their greatest hour of need. He will supply us with food, shelter and clothing. He also will provide us with support, guidance and direction about how to prepare and live during that time, both in business and in our personal life. He's not going to feed us with filet mignon, but he will give us all the necessary food we need to survive. Jesus says he knows what we need even before we ask, and that's all the assurance we need.

However, having a long-term miraculous supply of every need can become a soul-damning experience.

Consider what happened to the children of Israel in the desolate wilderness. For forty long years they lacked nothing. Angels' food fell from heaven. Water gushed out of a rock. Their tents never deteriorated or showed any wear-and-tear in all those years. Their sandals, turbans and garments never wore out. God supernaturally protected them from the blazing sun with a cloud over their camp, an area where scorching 105-degree heat would have killed them. The Lord protected them against attacks from all their enemies.

While every nation surrounding Israel was in confusion and turmoil, God's people enjoyed daily bread, water, shelter and protection.

In short, God did everything for Israel in their hard

times that we hope and pray he'll do for us in these perilous days. Think about it. The Israelites were unemployed, with no means of support whatsoever. Yet all of their needs were met. God did everything for them, and he will do no less for us today. The Lord has already demonstrated his power toward his people, so he doesn't have to prove anything to us. We can know he will do it again.

In the midst of all the frightening news, we must hear the message of God's holy word that he promises to keep and preserve all who trust him. The same God who took such loving care of Israel in the wilderness will do no less for us today.

If personal security is your primary focus and all you can think about is how to survive the economic chaos, then you are headed for a life of misery and boredom.

I believe God wants us to do our part to prepare for the storm that's coming, but even if we have everything we could possibly need to ride out a serious economic meltdown — a ten-year supply of food, a country hideaway, our own well, a generator, a wood stove — we may have the wrong focus. We can be convinced we're set for life and yet miss the point entirely. If we want God's provision, but not his presence, we'll end up like the Israelites, restless, empty and eventually falling away from him. We'll be secure here on earth but unsure of eternity.

Over time, Israel grew bored with the simple provisions they received from the Lord's hand. They began to murmur and complain, questioning God's power and love toward them, even as they received his daily, miraculous care. May that not be the case with us, when the storm hits. Jesus warns us very clearly not to focus on concerns such as what and how we'll eat, what we'll wear or how we'll be sheltered. He says, "Is not the life more than meat, and the body than raiment [clothing]?" (Matthew 6:25).

Christ wants to say to us, "Your focus in hard times should not be on survival. It shouldn't be on having food, water or shelter. Your heavenly father already knows you need these things, and he's ready to provide them. No, your focus should be on your relationship with me. Make me your main focus; get your heart right with me, and all else will be taken care of. If you'll just watch out for your heart, I'll watch out for your basket."

We need to learn that God's presence is our protection. We simply won't be able to survive the coming days without having an intense craving for his daily presence. In those difficult times, we're simply going to have to know he is with us.

Moses knew full well that without God's presence, Israel would never make it through the perilous times that had befallen them. They had already corrupted themselves by eating, drinking and dancing naked before a golden calf. God was so angered by their blatant idolatry, he called them a hopelessly stiff-necked people. He told Moses, "...my wrath...wax hot against them...I (will) consume them..." (Exodus 32:10).

God spared Israel because of Moses' intercession on their behalf, but he did so with one awful condition. The Lord told Israel, "Yes, I'll let you go into the land of milk and honey. I'll even send an angel to lead you. I'll thwart all your enemies before you, but I won't be with you, Israel. My presence will no longer be in your midst."

When Moses heard this, he was grieved. He responded by pitching his tent outside the Israelites' camp, far away from the rest of the people, and there he began to intercede before the Lord. He prayed, "...this people have sinned a great sin, and have made them gods of gold" (Exodus 32:31).

Notice here that Moses distinguishes between Israel's two sins, first their "great sin" and second their making of an idol. Apparently, the first sin led to the next. So, what was this "great sin" that caused Israel to worship a golden idol?

Israel's great sin is still the great sin of God's people today: a lack of respect for the presence of the Lord in their personal lives. The people lightly esteemed God's holy presence in their midst. They didn't have a craving in their hearts for communion with him. They wanted his provisions, his protection, his salvation, but not his presence.

Millions of Christians today also have nothing more than a "legal" relationship with the Lord.

Multitudes of believers rightly say, "I have laid hold of God's promise of salvation by faith in Christ's finished work on the cross. Therefore, I am saved; I'm a believer." I don't dispute a word of that. In strictly legal terms, we are all secure as sons and daughters of God. We are adopted into his holy family, and we ought to find rest in that knowledge.

However, if all we have with God is a legal contract or covenant, we've missed the point. A legal contract alone can never lead to a desire for communion, or holiness, or to know the Lord in fullness. If our relationship with our heavenly father goes no farther than this contract, where is the affection that exists between child and father? Where is our deep longing to know and experience his love? Where is our craving for fellowship and communion with him?

Some time ago, a person gave me a sermon published

on the internet. It was a powerful, brilliant message by a preacher who leads a life of lawlessness. This man smokes and drinks openly, and every time he's seen in a restaurant, he has a beautiful actress on his arm. Yet what a sermon he has written. Its central message is "You have to reach down into your gut, pull up some faith, lay hold of the finished work of Christ for you, and not let anybody ever shake you from that."

His message is all true, but it is strictly legal. It says nothing about love, devotion, drawing near to God, desiring holiness. That's what makes this lawless man's message so empty. Anyone who is truly shut in with God, experiencing his gift of salvation daily, longs to be conformed to Christ's image. This can never happen strictly through legal means; it must happen through love, affection, communion. The fact is, no one who lives a lawless life ever wants to enter the Lord's presence because it would expose his sinful heart.

Israel had become so lacking in love and affection for their heavenly father, God now offered them only what they really wanted: a legal deal. He gave them a binding promise of salvation from destruction, a good life of blessings and an angel to guide them in their journey; but because they remained stiff-necked, having no desire or regard for intimacy with the Lord, he withdrew his presence from them completely.

Up to this time, God's promises to Israel were all a part of his love affair with them. He had told them, "I'll bring you out of Egypt and break your bonds. In turn, I just want you to love me with all of your heart." Those words were intimate, full of affection. Over time, they became nothing more than legal language to a nation of increasingly hardened people.

This is all some Christians want from God today, a legal promise. They want to be able to say, "Now that I've got my 'fire insurance,' and I know I'm not going to hell, I can live as I please." Then they live like devils, but what a surprise awaits these poor, blinded souls!

When the majority will be satisfied merely with surviving and hoping for deliverance from hell, God will have a precious remnant outside all religious systems who will seek him with their whole hearts.

Out of Moses' prayer of mourning came this cry: "[Lord,] if thy presence go not with me, carry us not up hence" (Exodus 33:15). What a powerful statement! Moses was saying, in essence, "Unless we can have your presence, Lord – face-to-face communion with you and direction from your lips – any legal promises will be in vain. We might as well let the journey end here. We'd rather die where we stand. Without your presence, we're just like the dead heathen around us. Oh, Father, it's your presence in and among us that makes us different.

"We thank you, God, for your gracious promises to take good care of us. We're grateful for your covenant promises to protect and provide for us in these days of judgment. We know you're faithful to command your angels to watch over us. But, Lord, we yearn for more than your security. We crave and long for your presence. We want to walk closely with you, to embrace you, to have times of intimacy with you."

During our trip to Israel, we visited with two saintly women from the Lutheran Sisterhood of Mary. This is the wonderful ministry founded by Basilea Schlink, who is now in her eighties and lives in Germany. The two sisters in Israel have a compound on the Mount of Olives where they've labored in ministry for the Lord for thirty-six years. I have known them for all of those years, and they are godly, precious women of the Lord.

When the Six Day War broke out in 1967, the sisters faced an immediate crisis. Their house was surrounded by the Jordanian army, which dug in for battle. One of the Jordanian military officials warned the sisters, "You'd better flee this house. The war is going to break out shortly, and there's going to be a lot of bombing. You'll be caught in the middle of it all."

The sisters prayed about their situation, and the Lord gave them the same word he gave Gideon. "Don't be afraid. I will be with you." So, under the Spirit's direction, they stored a small but adequate supply of food and water in the basement, and they moved downstairs to ride out the war.

Within days, the Israeli army invaded from the left, and the Jordanians remained dug in on the right. Suddenly, the sisters were caught in the middle of intense warfare as bullets and shells began flying overhead and landing all around them. They huddled together in the basement of their house, spending hours in prayer.

At one point the house itself was shelled. One shell dropped through the roof, causing the walls of the house to collapse. The only wall left standing bore a plaque with a scripture promising God's protection. Another shell landed in the house, but it didn't break through to the basement. Then another shell landed on a pile of carpets stored in a corner, causing no harm.

What blessed me most as the sisters told us this story was that throughout their ordeal, Jesus' presence became overwhelming to them. His Spirit filled the basement as they sat huddled in prayer, and soon all their fears vanished. In fact, the sisters said it was the most blessed experience of their lifetime.

These women had food, water and shelter, and they were protected from their enemies. No bullet or bomb could touch them. Yet even this supernatural provision in the worst of circumstances paled in the light of the glorious presence of Christ himself. The sisters testified to us, "In all of our years in Israel, those were the most precious hours we've ever spent, because Jesus manifested himself to us so clearly in that basement. We experienced his presence as we've never known it."

They ended up with a supernatural craving in their hearts for his presence, wanting more and more of him. Now, as they think back to their hard times, they don't think about the provision God gave them. They think about the revelation of Christ they received from heaven.

I believe that in the coming days of crisis, we're going to see manifestations of the presence of Jesus as no other generation has seen. The apostle Paul would be jealous if he could even get close to what we're going to witness.

The greatest need in Christ's church right now is for godly saints to seek a deeper craving for his presence in their hearts, their homes, their churches. We won't have this craving for him in hard times unless we pray for it now. It has to come to us in the secret closet, the "craving place," because only God's Spirit can create such a hunger in us.

Do you have a craving place? Do you have a trysting spot where you spend intimate times with your Lord? Do you have a room where you get alone with him and cry, "Father, I want more than just a legal deal with you. I want your presence in my life."

Don't continue down the legal path. Go the way of love. That is what our Lord wants for us in the coming storm!

Chapter Nine

Not Fully Trusting God

When the author of Hebrews tells us the just shall live by faith, he's talking about more than just the faith leading to salvation. He's saying that faith is crucial to our daily existence. It includes everything we are and do. In short, God's people are to live through both good and bad times by fully trusting their lives into his hands. Of one thing we can be sure: God has always kept and protected those who have fully trusted him in times of crisis. In the troubled times ahead, we are going to need a settled and firm faith, for by no other means can we please God.

Paul admonished Timothy, "(Hold) faith, and a good conscience; which some having put away concerning faith have made shipwreck" (1 Timothy 1:19). Paul knew that when we face life's problems with unbelief, we end up floundering in despair. This is why Jude wrote to those living in the last days, "But ye, beloved, building up yourselves on your most holy faith, praying in the Holy Ghost" (Jude 1:20). Jude was saying, "You're going to need a healthy faith in the final hour, so start building up your faith right now."

This present hour on earth is no time to have a wavering faith. On the contrary, it is a time to lay hold of faith, and to build up your confidence in the Lord through diligent prayer and the study of his word. Otherwise, the events that are coming upon the world are going to totally swamp you. When the storm begins to rage and the winds of panic whip all around you, you'll be tempted to fear, and you could end up shipwrecked on the jagged rocks of bitterness. At this very hour, in economically depressed nations, the faith of many believers is being severely tested. From what I hear, the hard times have only strengthened the faith of most Christians.

Our spiritual fathers knew the kind of faith that is required in such an hour. David writes, "Our fathers trusted in thee: they trusted, and thou didst deliver them. They cried unto thee, and were delivered: they trusted in thee, and were not confounded" (Psalm 22:4-5).

Our forefathers weren't confused by all the storms that came upon them. They knew God would faithfully make a way for them.

One of these trusting fathers David referred to was Abraham. Paul writes of the father of our faith, "He staggered not at the promise of God through unbelief; but was strong in faith, giving glory to God; and being fully persuaded that, what he had promised, he was able also to perform" (Romans 4:20-21). Paul sets Abraham before us as an example of someone who fully trusted God, a man who was convinced the Lord would be faithful to fulfill his word in spite of all evidence to the contrary.

We would all like to have that kind of faith, never weak or wavering, always fully persuaded, with all doubts conquered. Such faith is not gained easily. This kind of strong faith comes only after we have endured testing after testing and failure after failure. Even Abraham did not receive his "faith name" until he came into a mature faith. He remained Abram up to the time that his faith was fully tested and proven to be grounded.

Peter encourages us to endure the trials of our faith, which come to every believer. "That the trial of your faith, being much more precious than of gold that perisheth, though it be tried with fire, might be found unto praise and honour and glory at the appearing of Jesus Christ" (1 Peter 1:7). The apostle adds that those who endure the fires of hard and difficult times will emerge as a people who "...are kept by the power of God through faith unto salvation ready to be revealed in the last time" (1 Peter 1:5).

In the last days, God is going to reveal just such a body of people, a remnant of faithful servants who have an absolutely unshakable faith. Their example of living by faith without a hint of fear in perilous times will be a testimony to the whole world. Faith is a call to abandon oneself to the steadfast promises of God.

Abram was a good, upright man who started out his journey of faith with a simple, trusting obedience. When the Lord commanded him, "...Get thee out of thy country, and from thy kindred, and from thy father's house, unto a land that I will shew thee" (Genesis 12:1), Abram went without question.

This is always where faith begins, with a call to abandon oneself to the will and leading of the Lord. God told Abram simply, "Go. I'll show you the way." He didn't tell Abram where he would lead him; he didn't name a country or a destination. Nor did God mention any of the awful hardships Abram was going to face along the way. He simply told Abram to leave his comfort zone and take a leap of faith into the arms of his heavenly father.

God said to him, in essence, "Abram, you're going to be

led into a whole new way of living. You've lived the good life so far. You've been settled and comfortable. But now you're going to have to face unsettling times and deprivations. There's no need to worry, because I'll give you step-by-step direction. You have to fully trust every step of this new path to me."

This calling was no small thing to Abram. He had a lot of responsibilities. He had a family, servants and a huge herd of cattle. Now he was being asked to pull up stakes and venture out into the unknown. It wasn't a light matter to step blindly into such a faith walk, having no idea where he was going. Yet that's the specific call Abram received from God.

The Lord gave Abram this promise: "I'm going to make you the father of a whole different race of people. You're going to give rise to a people who will walk as you walk, completely by faith. This great nation is going to come out of your loins, and I'm going to bless you and make your name great. In fact, you're going to be a blessing to every nation." (see Genesis 12:2).

When God promised Abram that every family of the earth would be blessed through him, he was speaking of Christ. Abram was going to be the first of a new race of trusting people whom God had desired since the beginning of creation. When the Lord called Abram to walk by faith, he was laying a foundation for this new race. They were to be a people who would live by faith, just as Abram did. They were to find salvation by faith, they were to be counted as righteous by faith, and they were to overcome every hardship by faith. Their ultimate example of faith would come later in Christ.

Today we can see down the road of Abram's future. We know he was going to need faith to believe God to do the impossible. He absolutely had to rely on the miraculous to believe that an old, impotent man like himself would conceive a child with his no longer fertile wife. Simply put, he had to believe for a miraculous conception to take place, an absolute impossibility according to human thinking.

That wasn't all. The time would come when his seed would have to believe a sea would be opened up, allowing an entire nation of people to walk through it on dry ground. They would have to believe that angels' food would fall from the sky to feed God's people in a dead, dry wilderness and that they would drink water flowing out of a rock.

All of these things were humanly impossible, yet God's people would have to believe him to provide them all, if they were to survive. Abram was to be the father of this believing, trusting race of people. This meant he had to have a strong faith himself.

You might think Abram possessed this kind of faith. Think of the faith it took for him to abandon himself into God's hands, merely to start such a journey into the unknown. He was already seventy-five years old, and his wife, Sarah, was in her sixties. They were going to have to travel more than three hundred miles through the desert, facing a blazing sun, scorching heat, wild animals and few watering holes. You couldn't tell Abram his walk of faith was going to be easy.

Today, in our naiveté, we casually ask, "What was the secret to Abram's faith? What was his theology of trusting God?" We discuss his faith, dissect it and analyze all the scripture passages about him. Yet if we were to ask Abram what faith is, I believe he would tell us, "Faith is simply trusting your life and future fully into God's care and leading. My Lord told me, 'Go, Abram. I'll show you the way.' So I got up and followed. It was nothing complicated. I simply obeyed his call to yield my life completely to his hands."

You and I today have received this same calling of faith. The author of Hebrews writes, "The just shall live by faith…" (Hebrews 10:38). I believe Abram's response to God's calling exemplifies the scriptural definition of faith. "…he went out, not knowing whither he went" (Hebrews 11:8). We face life-changing times which demand that, like Abram, we cast ourselves into the faithful arms of our Lord and trust him to lead us through the coming days of trial.

Have you stepped out to face the future in faith, not knowing what lies ahead? It doesn't matter how uncertain things look, or how hard your circumstances may seem. Eventually, everyone who would follow Jesus has to come to a place where he says, "Lord, I'm stepping out. I'm laying down all my own ideas on how to live, how to be blessed, how to lead my family, how to provide a living. I'm putting all of that in your hands, and I'm trusting your guidance. You determine my every step."

What do you get when you commit to a walk of faith, surrendering all to God's will and leading?

You get more trouble, more testing! What happens when you make the kind of commitment Abram did? You face the most intense trials you've ever known. What was the result of Abram's decision to follow God's calling? He ended up in the middle of a severe famine. When he arrived in Canaan, God told him, "This is it, Abram. Here's the land I'm going to give to your family. Your sons will inherit it all. Go ahead and walk from one end to the other. Every step of it is yours."

Abram did just that, but all he saw was a withered, barren landscape. The trees were dying. Water for the cattle was scarce. There was no pasture, nothing to provide for him and his family. The Bible says, "...the famine was grievous in the land" (Genesis 12:10).

Abram probably thought, "Lord, I don't know if I want this..." I imagine him saying to Sarah, "I think I heard the wrong voice. It couldn't have been God leading me. There's nothing here. There's no food to give our family or even grass for the cattle. How could this dry, unfulfilling place be my reward for obedience? After all my prayers to the Lord, my diligent seeking of his face, my total obedience to his will, how could it lead to this famine? Where did I miss God? How did I get out of his will?"

Scripture tells us Abram then built an altar and called on God. Judging by his later actions, we can guess how he might have prayed. "Lord, I obeyed you. I trusted your leading, leaving my comfort zone by faith, never knowing what lay ahead of me. You promised you would bless my obedience. Yet now, after all my hardships to get here, I find there's no blessing in this land at all. My walk with you is nothing but a difficult test."

Have you ever prayed this way? You know your heart burns with love for the Lord. You walk in covenant with him, surrendered to his will and obedient to his leading. He has led you very clearly to this present point in your life. After all your faithful obedience, your devoted prayer life, your constant cry for holiness, he has brought you into a crisis that makes absolutely no sense. It seems contrary to everything you know about the Lord and his word.

Perhaps you finally got that better-paying job you'd

been praying for, and you gave the Lord thanks for honoring your faith. Within a short time, though, your coveted job got downsized. Suddenly, you're out of work altogether, wondering how you're going to provide for your needs.

Maybe you've just been told a family member has inoperable cancer. You cry out, "Lord, I've been walking faithfully before you for years, doing everything you've asked. Is this the reward of my faith, that my family has to face this kind of torturous trial?"

Perhaps you know a devoted, godly woman who has trusted the Lord for years to bring a spiritual man into her life. Finally, she met a man she believed God had sent. He seemed so right for her. But after a long, steady courtship, he suddenly walked away from her without giving any reason why.

It doesn't matter who you are or how devoted you've been. You may be a holy servant of the Lord, obedient, prayerful, walking in the full measure of the faith you've been given. God may still lead you into the greatest test of faith possible.

This is just what happened to Abram. He was a pure, holy, God-loving, obedient servant. Yet God led him directly into an awful experience, a dreaded famine. In Abram's day, a person couldn't encounter anything worse. Famines brought fear, destruction, starvation, death.

So it is today. Like the rest of the world, the trusting saints of God are soon going to be led into a different sort of famine, a global depression marked by deprivation and suffering. Our faith is going to go into the fire, and we will be severely tested. Out of this fiery test, the faith of many will come forth as pure gold.

Whatever measure of faith Abram had up to this time, it still lacked a certain dimension. The famine crisis demanded of Abram an even bigger leap of faith than it took for him to set out on his journey. Like Israel at the banks of the Red Sea, Abram saw before him a humanly impossible situation. Only a miracle could save him. His very life was at stake, as were the lives of his wife, children, extended family and servants. There simply was no way for them to survive.

Let me remind you here of Satan's accusation to God about Job. "Skin for skin, yea, all that a man hath will he give for his life. But put forth thine hand now, and touch his bone and his flesh, and he will curse thee to thy face" (Job 2:4-5). The devil makes this same accusation against all of God's people today. He says, "Sure, they'll trust you, God, up to the time their bellies are empty. Just put them in a hard place and see how much faith they have in you. Send a depression on them. When they begin to feel the pain and their survival is threatened, they'll curse you to your face!"

At this point, Abram either had to believe God for the impossible – to move into a realm of trust in the miraculous – or to take matters into his own hands. Did he pass the test? No, he failed miserably. The Bible says, "...Abram went down into Egypt to sojourn there..." (Genesis 12:10). He didn't stand still to see the Lord work out his deliverance. He didn't take a leap of faith that required him to trust God for the impossible. Instead, he made his own plans for survival.

The Psalms reveal God's heart toward his people in just such a crisis. "Behold, the eye of the Lord is upon them that fear him...to deliver their soul from death, and to keep them alive in famine" (Psalm 33:18-19). "...in the days of famine they shall be satisfied" (Psalm 37:19). God already had a plan to keep Abram and his family through the famine. They were in absolutely no danger. God planned to feed and protect them by incredible miracles.

Faith begins with a total abandonment of oneself into God's care; but our faith must be active, not passive. We must have full confidence that God can and will do the impossible. Jesus said, "...with God all things are possible" (Matthew 19:26). "With God nothing shall be impossible" (Luke 1:37). In short, faith says, "God is enough."

The Lord was making Abram a man of faith by leading him into an impossible situation. He wanted to hear his servant say, "Father, you led me here, and you know best, so I'm going to stand still and believe you to do the impossible. I'll put my life in your hands, fully trusting that you won't allow me or my family to starve. I know we'll be preserved because you promised I would have a seed." But fear and doubt overwhelmed Abram. Instead, his cry was, "Lord, get me out of here!"

Our faith is not meant to get us out of a hard place or change our painful condition. Rather, it is meant to reveal God's faithfulness to us in the midst of our dire situation. God does occasionally change our trying circumstances, but more often he doesn't because he wants to change us.

We simply can't trust God's power fully until we experience it in the midst of our crisis. This was the case with the three Hebrew children. They saw Christ only when they were in the midst of the fiery furnace. Daniel experienced God's power and grace after he was thrust into the lions' den. If they had suddenly been pulled out of their circumstances, they never would have known the full grace of God's miracle-working power. The Lord would not have been magnified before the ungodly.

We see examples of this also in the New Testament. Even when a storm hit the disciples' boat, Jesus remained fast asleep. Soon water began to flood over the sides, and it looked as if the boat would sink. That's when Christ's panic-stricken disciples woke their master. Jesus stood up and merely spoke a word, "Peace," and the storm abruptly ended. His disciples were amazed at this display of God's supernatural power.

They missed an even greater display of God's power, though. The greater miracle was that this man was fully at peace, able to sleep through a life-or-death crisis, because he was totally at rest in his father's care. Jesus knew his father had promised that he would be the redeemer of the world. He knew God would keep his promise.

We think we're witnessing great miracles whenever God ends our storms and crises, but we can easily miss the lesson of faith in such times, the lesson that says God will remain faithful to us through our hard times. He wants to raise us above our trials through faith, so we can say, "My God can do the impossible. He's a deliverer, and he's going to keep me. I can sleep through any storm."

When Abram went down to Egypt, he was telling God, in essence, "Okay, Lord, I'll take it from here." He presumed his flesh had made a mistake, that he'd heard the wrong voice; and now he had to take it upon himself to straighten things out. This is where Abram left the path of faith. He gathered his brood together and said, "We're getting out of here. I don't know where I missed it, but we just can't make it here. We're going to Egypt."

The good news is that our failures often lead us to develop a strong faith. Nevertheless, we face consequences whenever we leave the path of faith and operate in the flesh. Let me name a few of these consequences.

If we turn to our flesh, we soon find ourselves trying to manipulate both people and circumstances in order to survive. Abram did this as he concocted a scheme for surviving the hostile Egyptians. When he and his entourage came to Egypt's border, Abram told Sarah, "You're a beautiful woman, and the Egyptian men are going to want you. They'll try to kill me so they can take you for themselves, but you'll save my life if you tell just a little white lie. If you pretend you're my sister, we'll all be safe." (Sarah was indeed Abram's half sister.)

Those who walk in the flesh are self-centered, always looking out for number one; but the person who trusts God fully, believing him for the impossible, knows he doesn't need human resources. He doesn't need to manipulate things, make excuses or push forward his personal agenda. Rather, he surrenders himself totally to God's will and leaves all results to him.

Abram had not yet come to this point. He would get there eventually and become the father of faith, just as God desired. Abram's faith, though, had to grow out of his failure. The Lord was building something important in his servant through this experience.

By not fully trusting God, we literally put other people's lives at risk. By telling a "white lie," Abram put his wife's life in danger. When he told the Egyptians that Sarah was his sister, they took Sarah into Pharaoh's harem. It was only through God's supernatural protection that Sarah wasn't defiled sexually by the heathen ruler. Worse, had Sarah been impregnated by Pharaoh, she would have given birth to a heathen seed, not the promised seed through whom the whole world would be blessed.

God plagued Pharaoh's house until the ruler realized

something was amiss. Soon Pharaoh reasoned, "This is all happening because of that Hebrew woman. She's a follower of Jehovah God." Pharaoh called Abram on the carpet, demanding, "Why didn't you tell us she was your wife?" Immediately he had Abram and Sarah unceremoniously thrust out of the country, as any common deceiver would be.

Abram had abused God's honor. Now his own testimony was ruined. Because of his deceitful actions, he had turned off the Egyptians to anything he could have testified about the Lord. The same thing happens today whenever a man or woman of God tries to establish his or her own righteousness.

Are you trying to manipulate things to make something happen in your life? Do you think you've heard from God wrongly because things aren't happening as he promised? No, you haven't heard wrong. You're just in the midst of the trial God has ordained for you, and he's urging you to turn to him in faith right now.

As the storm clouds gather over America and other nations even now and all our futures look uncertain, the voice of God's Spirit cries out to each of his children, "The just shall live by faith!"

CHAPTER TEN

THE SECRET TO STRENGTH

In the book of Leviticus, Moses describes the fearful condition Israel would fall into when God's judgments began to fall upon the earth. According to Leviticus 26:36-37, three things would happen.

First, the Lord would send a faintness upon the people's hearts.

Second, the people would become so panic-stricken, they would run at the sound of a shaking leaf.

Third, they would have no power to stand before their enemies.

These things could very well happen throughout America. Consider what happens on Wall Street and in our financial institutions whenever a mere rumor of bad news is heard. It's cause enough to send the stock market into a tailspin. Whenever an economic expert or government leader issues a single negative word about the economy, the market begins to tremble and fluctuate wildly. Traders and brokers hang on these leaders' every word, hoping to hear about some solution that will rescue the market from the inevitable disaster it's headed toward.

I believe Moses' prophecy was meant not only for ancient Israel but for God's people throughout history. For weeks during the autumn of 1998, the New York Times included photos of stockbrokers and businesspeople around the globe – Indonesia, Korea, Japan, Russia – bowed down in despair in front of stock market boards. They're pictured holding their heads in their hands, their eyes hollow, their spirits devastated by fear. You can see the panic and terror in their expressions as they face the inevitable.

All the terrible things we see taking place in the world were summed up in a warning Jesus gave. "There shall be signs in the sun, and in the moon, and in the stars; and upon the earth distress of nations, with perplexity; the sea and the waves roaring; men's hearts failing them for fear, and for looking after those things which are coming on the earth: for the powers of heaven shall be shaken" (Luke 21:25-26).

Think about Jesus' descriptions here. Now think about all the devastating events that have been reported from around the world. These days you may hear talk from Wall Street brokers and traders that sounds cool and nonchalant. Some observers claim, "We can ride it out. We've survived every other crash in history. And now we can beat this one, too." Moses told the truth bluntly about all this tough talk. He prophesied people would melt into puddles of water when the storm hits, that they would be panicking, trembling, fainting at the sound of such ominous news.

What does God's word prophesy about the righteous when his judgments begin to fall on the land?

David prophesies in very clear terms. The righteous, obedient, godly person "...shall not be afraid of evil tidings: his heart is fixed, trusting in the Lord. His heart is established, he shall not be afraid..." (Psalm 112:7-8). Let me paraphrase this passage for Christians living in these perilous times: "No one who trusts his whole being to the Lord will be troubled by any of the coming bad news."

Isaiah 34 gives us an incredible picture of God's sword of wrath striking the nations of the earth. The prophet tells us, "For the indignation of the Lord is upon all nations...for it is the day of the Lord's vengeance..." (Isaiah 34:2, 8).

In the next chapter, Isaiah abruptly stops his description of God's awful judgments. Suddenly, in the midst of delivering these terrible tidings, he brings a word of comfort to God's trembling people. "Strengthen ye the weak hands, and confirm the feeble knees. Say to them that are of a fearful heart, Be strong, fear not: behold, your God will come with vengeance, even God with a recompense; he will come and save you" (Isaiah 35:3-4).

What a profound, uplifting word! God is saying to his people, "Yes, my sword of vengeance is going to bring every wicked nation to ruin, but it is not meant to harm you. In the coming days, you'll see me smiting the nations and dealing harshly with sin. But you are not to fear. Although my judgments will humble your nation, they will also serve as your salvation. As the wicked become weaker and weaker with fear, you will become stronger and stronger through your communion with me. Your confidence in me will grow continually. Lift up your heads, saints. You have no reason to fear."

This is God's hope and desire for all of his people in perilous times. We hear it in Paul's admonishment. "Watch ye, stand fast in the faith, quit you like men, be strong" (1 Corinthians 16:13). We also read it in Paul's letter to the Ephesians. "Finally, my brethren, be strong in the Lord, and in the power of his might" (Ephesians 6:10). God wants us to face the coming dark days with a spiritual strength that will withstand every evil report.

You can be certain the Lord will have this kind of strong, trusting body of believers to glorify him in these hard times. Already we're witnessing the steadfast faith of saints who are having to endure trials and tribulations in depressed countries. Their vibrant faith shines through the darkness like beacons of holy light.

As news of disorder and distress breaks on a larger scale, all of America will tremble. People will sense the signs of economic difficulty, yet our Lord is going to have a great testimony in just such a time. While most Americans are panicking and drowning in the storm, God's holy remnant will stand out as a beacon of peace and assurance. Their peace will be their testimony. They won't have to pass out tracts, carry their Bibles or even testify to prove they're Christians. Their countenances will be so full of God's supernatural peace, everyone around them will know they possess something different.

People will ask these saints, "How can you smile in such a time? What kind of investment did you make that allows you to be so happy?" God's servants will answer, "I've got a bank you know nothing about!" What is this bank? It is God's promise to all of his children, "Even when you're standing in the midst of my swirling vengeance, I will save you and keep you from all harm!"

Sadly, many lukewarm Christians are going to faint, fret and despair as they hear the bad news mounting daily. The reports will be so ominous and frightful, these believers will react in the same way as the ungodly. They'll tremble, quaking at the "sound of a shaking leaf." Their faith will waver, and they'll be carried away by the spirit of fear that grips the world. In fact, some will be among that great number of people who literally die of fright.

We'll see trembling as well among the multitudes of ministers who have drifted far from Jesus in their daily walk. Sin and compromise have robbed them of all spiritual power and authority. They won't be prepared to deliver a sure word to their sheep when it's most needed. Instead, their congregations will sit in stunned silence as they watch their shaken pastors grope for words in the pulpit like blind men.

The news of our nation's fall will be so unbelievable, so frightening, these compromising shepherds won't know what to say. Everyone in their churches will look at each other through eyes of fear, hoping it's all a bad dream. I tell you, being in such a church will be like sitting in a funeral parlor.

There is a holy remnant of believers who have learned the secret of getting and maintaining strength in these perilous times. When that awful day comes, God's righteous remnant will know how to maintain their strength. It won't matter to them if the moon and stars fall from the sky or if the mountains quake and fall into the sea. They will still have faith in Christ to deliver them, and their faith won't be shaken.

In Psalm 31, David introduces us to the phrase "the secret of thy presence." He writes, "Oh how great is thy goodness, which thou hast laid up for them that fear thee; which thou hast wrought for them that trust in thee before the sons of men! Thou shalt hide them in the secret of thy presence from the pride of man: thou shalt keep them secretly in a pavilion from the strife of tongues" (Psalm 31:19-20).

David is saying something very profound here. "All true

strength comes from drawing near to the Lord. The measure of our strength is proportionate to our nearness to him." Simply put, the closer we are to Jesus, the stronger we're going to be. All the strength we're ever going to need will come only through our secret life of prayer. If we'll just draw near to Christ, he will draw near to us, giving us a fresh supply of strength daily. This is the secret of his presence.

In the Old Testament, the presence of the Lord was associated with the ark. Israel believed that wherever the ark was, God's presence was there. Wherever the people traveled, they took the ark along with them. We see an example of this faith concerning the Lord's presence with the ark in 1 Samuel 4.

At the time, Israel was losing a military battle with the Philistines. God's people had already suffered some 4,000 casualties. Now their leaders wondered, "Why are we losing this battle? Why are we being smitten before the enemy?" Finally, someone realized, "The Lord's presence is not with us. Quick, go get the ark. We need God's presence with us in this battle." "Let us fetch the ark of the covenant of the Lord out of Shiloh unto us, that, when it cometh among us, it may save us out of the hand of our enemies" (1 Samuel 4:3).

When the ark came within sight of the Israelites' camp, the soldiers "...shouted with a great shout, so that the earth rang again" (1 Samuel 4:5). As the Philistines heard this noise, they wondered, "What does this mean?" Suddenly, they grew fearful. "...they understood that the ark of the Lord was come into the camp. And the Philistines were afraid, for they said, God is come into the camp. And they said, Woe unto us!..." (1 Samuel 4:6-7).

This passage provides a vivid illustration of the battle

being waged against God's church today. It reveals much about the strategy of our enemy, Satan. The devil greatly fears the Lord's presence in our lives. He trembles at the very thought of a believer's nearness to Christ. So, when his demonic hordes see you on your knees each day, in the presence of your heavenly father, all of hell cries out, "Woe is us! God is with this believer. He has the divine presence. What can we do against him now?"

This is why Satan will do everything in his power to rob you of the Lord's presence in your life. It's why he wants to bog down your soul in rebellion and sin. He wants you drained of all strength. He'll try to put you in the lap of some Delilah to cut off your source of power. He may tempt you to become sidetracked into some busy pursuit or even some time-consuming ministry. He'll use anything he can, even "good" things, to keep you away from spending time alone with Jesus. He knows your time with Christ makes you invincible to the fears and anxieties of this age.

As the ark was carried into Israel's camp, the Israelite soldiers cried at the top of their lungs, "The Lord is with us! Victory is ours now. The enemy is defeated." As it turned out, however, Israel was routed by the Philistines in an awful slaughter. They ended up fleeing for their lives. Worst of all, the ark was captured by the Philistines. Why did this happen? How could the promise of God's presence turn into such a terrible defeat?

Tragically, God had already removed his presence from his house in Shiloh, and his Spirit had left the ark as well. Neither of these places represented his presence among his people anymore. At this point, there was nothing left of his glory in Israel but an abandoned temple and an empty relic of God's departed presence.

Sadly, the doctrine of God's presence among his people was no longer a living reality in Israel. It had become a dry, dead theology because the people's hearts had drifted far from him. Eli, the high priest at the time, was a compromised, backslidden shepherd over Israel. His sons conducted an adulterous, pleasure-mad ministry. Together, their effect on the nation was devastating. No one cared about having the Lord's presence anymore. They only wanted his power. They may have thought God's presence was with them, but it was only a delusion. They had sinned away his presence completely.

I would think that everyone reading this book is convinced that we will face very difficult times. You'd have to be totally blind not to see the chastening that's coming to America and the world. The national news networks are using the phrase "global depression" for the first time. The world may be finally acknowledging we will eventually and inevitably face widespread economic hardship. As a believer, you are faced with an important question: How near to Jesus are you?

I believe that when things begin to disintegrate, the most powerful testimony for Christ will be the believer whose heart is wholly at peace.

While the rest of society is panicking, fainting, dying from fear, the overcoming Christian will be growing stronger and stronger, receiving continual encouragement from the Holy Spirit.

If you want to be able to stand in this manner when the storm hits, you must have the Lord's presence in your life daily. How near is the Lord to you? Are you growing closer to him with each passing day? How much quality time do you spend alone with him? When you're with him, are you able to say, "Master, I'm in no hurry. This is my time with you, and nothing else will take your place in this hour."

You may answer, "I think I'm prepared for the storm. After all, I'm a faithful witness for the Lord. I'm not ashamed of the gospel. I live a clean, moral life. I tithe; I read my Bible, and I attend church regularly." That's all fine, yet you can do all those things and be distant from the Lord. If you don't spend time alone with him, it doesn't matter how much you witness. Your words will have no power, no results. Your testimony will be dead because you've drifted away from your source of strength.

Don't make the mistake of measuring your walk with Jesus by your good works rather than by his presence in your life. You can't be more pleasing to the Lord or more fulfilled and at the center of his will than by shutting yourself in with him in prayer.

Paul faced many hard, perilous times. He knew what it meant to lose everything, to hunger, to thirst, to suffer deprivation, to be abandoned, to lie chained in a dark, damp prison cell, alone and forsaken by his close friends. Yet Paul never fainted. In fact, he grew stronger through every trial. How? He knew the secret to getting and maintaining true strength. Paul lived so near to Jesus that he could say, "Christ has possessed me, taken me over. He now actually lives in me."

The apostle testified, "At my first answer no man stood with me, but all men forsook me: I pray God that it may not be laid to their charge. Notwithstanding the Lord stood with me, and strengthened me...And the Lord shall deliver me from every evil work, and will preserve me unto his heavenly kingdom: to whom be glory for ever and ever" (2 Timothy 4:16-18).

Paul knew that if he stayed near the Lord, Christ would

honor him by standing with him. He said, "Everywhere I turned, there was trouble and distress. Yet, when everybody let me down, when I was alone and all I could see was hard times, the Lord came to me and poured strength into me. He delivered me from the devil's trap. He gave me an assurance he would keep me from every evil work, and he will continue to keep me until I get to heaven."

You can't obtain this kind of assurance and strength anywhere but in the presence of the Lord himself. Paul waited on the Lord continually. He was in constant communion with him. That's why no evil news or trials could shake him. Each time he faced another terrible trial, he escaped to prayer, running to Jesus to unburden his heart.

When Paul uses the word "notwithstanding" in the above passage, he means, "in spite of." He's saying, "The Lord stood with me and strengthened me in spite of all the evil conditions around me." Paul thrilled to see his spiritual children grasping this idea of "notwithstanding" in their lives. He saw the Lord strengthen them to stand in even the most difficult times.

Paul praised these believers, saying, "...ye endured a great fight of afflictions...ye were made a gazingstock both by reproaches and afflictions...(you) took joyfully the spoiling of your goods..." (Hebrews 10:32-34). He was reminding them, "When anybody else would have been screaming at God and gnashing their teeth, you were growing stronger. The Holy Spirit was strengthening you through it all."

These people lost their homes, their livelihoods, everything. They could testify along with their pastor, "Notwithstanding the hard times, in spite of them all, the Lord stood with us. He came daily to give us all the strength we needed to overcome." Do you have a "notwithstanding" in your life? Have you come to the place where you can say, "In spite of it all, I know if I stay close to Jesus in these hard times that he will give me everything I need. He is my source of strength."

Paul learned this secret of strength at his conversion. After being blinded on the road to Damascus, he spent three days fasting and praying. He was so determined to know this Lord who had revealed himself to him, he refused all bodily comforts. It was then God commanded a believer named Ananias, "Go, minister to Paul." "...for, behold, he prayeth" (Acts 9:11). Scripture next says of Paul, "Saul increased the more in strength..." (Acts 9:22). Paul remained in prayer the whole time, and God continually met him with strength upon strength.

We see this truth illustrated also in Jesus' parable of the man who seeks bread from his friend at midnight. The man had no bread himself, but he knew his friend had all the bread he needed. He kept pounding and knocking on the door until his friend gave him bread. Beloved, that friend with the bread is Jesus. He sticks closer than a brother, and he will supply us with everything we need. This includes not only food, clothing and shelter (see Matthew 6) but also encouragement, strength and anointing.

However, God will not give any of these things to those who treat his presence casually. If you come home from work, flop on the sofa, flip on the TV and waste away the hours, don't expect to receive anything from him. If you spend more time on the golf course than you do on your knees, you will never gain true strength. There is no source of strength outside the presence of the Lord.

How are you preparing for the evil tidings, the bombardment of bad news? What are you doing to get ready for the hour of affliction and the possible spoiling of your earthly goods?

I had a conversation with a friend in east Texas who raises cattle and crops. He described to me the ruinous effects the long drought had on Texas during 1998. Then, he said, toward the end of the summer, the area received twelve inches of rain, causing floods. Now another drought was being forecast. To make things worse, my friend told me, the land was being invaded by army worms. One day he looked out his window and saw that his green fields had turned yellow. When he walked outside to inspect the crops, he realized the plants had been devoured down to the stalks. He told me, "Talk about plagues and pestilences. We've had drought, then floods, then more drought. Now everything is being eaten up by worms."

Soon our conversation turned to the multibillion-dollar bailout of Long-Term Capital. We talked for a while about the dire signs on the financial landscape. Half an hour later, as I hung up the phone, it dawned on me how nonchalantly we had been discussing these awful calamities.

That's when I knew we're not ready. We think we are, but we treat the subject of economic ruin lightly. We shrug our shoulders and say, "All we can do is trust the Lord and try to make it through the best we can. There's nothing more we can do than that."

There is something we can do. Indeed, there is a certain, specific preparation we all should be making right now. We need to start building up our faith and spiritual strength, and the only way to do that is by drawing near to Jesus in our secret closet of prayer. We simply won't get this strength in any other way. David instructs us, "...them that trust in thee before the sons of men...thou shalt hide them in the secret of thy presence..." (Psalm 31:19-20).

It's time to shut ourselves in with Christ and pour out our hearts to him daily. When the fury of the coming storm strikes, you're going to need your own supply of strength. You won't be able to make it on the strength of anyone else, not your mate, your pastor, your friend or even a prophet.

When the Lord judged Israel, the people thought they could run to the prophets to save them. But God told them, "Though these three men, Noah, Daniel, and Job, were in it, they should deliver but their own souls by their righteousness, saith the Lord God" (Ezekiel 14:14). God was warning Israel, "Even these godly men had only enough righteousness to deliver themselves. Not even the most righteous person today has enough to save you."

We see this same truth illustrated in Jesus' parable of the foolish virgins. When these virgins tried to borrow oil from their wise counterparts, they were told, "Go buy oil for yourselves. We don't have enough for us and you too." Do you hear what Jesus himself is saying in this parable? He's warning us, "No one else has enough faith to carry you. You have to have your own."

Let me now address all Christian wives. One day soon, when the world is coming down all around you, your praying husband will not be able to calm your troubled, fearful spirit. You may see him getting stronger as you begin to melt in fear and terror, but he won't be able to help you. You need your own supply of strength! You can't get it by merely listening to sermons or teaching tapes. You can't get it by only being involved in corporate worship or by doing good works. You can only get it by being alone in the Lord's presence.

I now direct the same message to all Christian husbands. You may think you can rely on your devoted wife to pray you out of fear, but your mate could be called home during the hard times ahead. What will you do then, when you realize you've placed all your hope and security in her? You'll be so stricken with panic by the perilous times, you'll be blinded.

Singles and career people, I beg you to begin seeking the Lord wholeheartedly. If you'll start spending time alone with your Lord daily, your knees won't ever tremble, no matter how frightening the news becomes. You won't fear the loss of job or home because you'll have the assurance of your savior to supply you.

I speak now to every Christian. The time has come for you to get alone with Jesus, to seek his face and develop a loving relationship with him in prayer.

The psalmist says of those who appear before the Lord in Zion, "They go from strength to strength..." (Psalm 84:7). He's telling us, "The praying believer will not faint in hard times. On the contrary, he'll grow stronger and stronger because he trusts in God before the sons of men."

Isaiah gives us these powerful words: "Hast thou not known? Hast thou not heard, that the everlasting God, the Lord, the Creator of the ends of the earth, fainteth not, neither is weary? There is no searching of his understanding. He giveth power to the faint; and to them that have no might he increaseth strength. Even the youths shall faint and be weary, and the young men shall utterly fall: but they that wait upon the Lord shall renew their strength; they shall mount up with wings as eagles; they shall run, and not be weary; and they shall walk, and not faint" (Isaiah 40:28-31).

Chapter Eleven

Awakened Through Suffering

As I read the scriptures, I see hope revealed for God's church in the midst of the coming troubles. I believe that during this time of judgment, the Lord is going to purge and awaken his people. Financial ruin will certainly be a part of the judgment that lies ahead. According to God's word, judgment begins in his house, but will God revive his people in this time of purging and judgment?

We can't answer that until we define what the church is. I believe the true church of Jesus Christ is alive and well and wide awake. It is not an organization but a hidden body of devoted believers who have not wavered in their passion for Christ. It has never backslidden, grown cold or lukewarm, or compromised. This body is still moving and acting in the love and power of Christ. In fact, it is closer to Jesus than ever before, seated with him in heavenly places. If that is all true, how could such a church possibly need what Christians today so loosely call "revival"?

I also believe that much of what is called the church today is not recognized or accepted by God as "his" church. It is precisely this dead, sin-laden, cold church of man – not the church of God – that needs reviving. In the coming days, this backslidden church will be the target of God's purging and chastening. Right now, it is a church being deceived by ministers who act as predators, preying on widows, the poor and the spiritually uninformed. They have misled multitudes with their message of prosperity, encouraging them to trust in a health-and-wealth gospel that totally misrepresents Jesus.

God has already written the obituaries for these false shepherds' ministries. In the coming depression, prosperity preachers are going to see the world falling down all around them. Evangelists who promoted a glitzy gospel and a Santa-Claus Christ are going to go bankrupt. Most tragic of all, when the prosperity vanishes and hard times set in, those who were bewitched by this phony gospel will end up trusting no one, not even the Lord.

Man's church must first be brought to ruin before God can rebuild anything good and acceptable from it.

God wants to restore the backslidden church. The prophet Hosea speaks of the Lord's hope for these people. "O Israel, return unto the Lord thy God; for thou hast fallen by thine iniquity" (Hosea 14:1). Hosea is telling God's people, "Prosperity has so hardened your heart, there's no other way the Lord can reach you but through judgment. You people are so backslidden and have turned so far from him, he's going to have to strip you of everything. Prepare for him to shake your lives to their very foundation. The only hope you'll have left is in turning to him just to survive."

When Hosea spoke these words, the storm was already upon Israel. God was chastening the nation, just as he said he would. A severe drought came upon the land, and all the springs of water dried up. Soon all the treasuries were depleted, and everything collapsed before the people's eyes. Nothing could stop the depression that swept through the country. Desolation and hard times fell upon Israel, and suddenly everyone was fearful, sorrowful, wailing like a woman in travail.

Today, God is giving the backslidden church a similar warning. He's saying, "You will face the very hardest of times. I'm going to shake everything you see, your economy, your savings, your possessions. When all the earthly things you've trusted in have been stripped away and all that's of the flesh is bankrupted, when all your institutions crumble and you have to struggle just to survive, maybe then you'll repent and turn to me." Then and only then, God says, "I will heal their backsliding, I will love them freely: for mine anger is turned away from him" (Hosea 14:4). God can heal the worldly institutional church, but I agree with Hosea. Healing can come only through the tearing down of all that has drawn people's hearts away from God, including the love of material things.

Jesus said, "...the gates of hell shall not prevail against (my church)" (Matthew 16:18). Isaiah tells us no weapon formed against God's people will prosper (see Isaiah 54:17). The Lord's devoted church has experienced the truth of these words firsthand, but the gates of hell are prevailing over the church of man. The word "prevail" here means "overpower, defeat." Satan has so overpowered and corrupted this worldly church that God no longer recognizes it as his.

Sadly, some denominations have been overpowered by the devil's weapons. How else could you describe what is happening in many liberal church organizations? Bishops are ordaining homosexuals. Ministers no longer believe the Bible is the living word of God. They say there was no virgin birth of Christ and that there is no heaven or hell. They call good evil and evil good. They advocate abortion. They loudly disclaim Christ's miracles. Now many church-affiliated colleges and seminaries are demeaning all that is holy. Their professors seem hell-bent on shipwrecking what little faith their young students have left. If this doesn't comprise a picture of the church being overpowered by the enemy, I don't know what does.

God has never acknowledged any such apostasy or foolishness as representing his church. This defeated, overpowered "church of man" may be highly esteemed by the world, but it remains an abomination in the eyes of the Lord. Indeed, this is the church that needs to be shaken and purified.

I believe most Christians don't have a clear understanding of what constitutes the true church of the Lord Jesus Christ. We have drifted too far away from any true definition of Christ's church.

For example, think of the carnal, fleshly ways we measure success in the church.

Most often, we calculate God's blessing by bigness and growth, in terms of both numbers and finances. We are awed by mega-churches, "fastest growing" churches, churches with every conceivable type of program. As we behold their grand edifices, their sprawling, multi-acre campuses and their sanctuaries packed with thousands of people, we can't help thinking, "That is a successful church. God must really be at work there."

I can assure you, though, God does not measure success by any of these standards. A church can have multiple thousands in attendance, a huge budget and great charitable outreaches, and Jesus still may not be in any of it.

Wherever flesh is at work, God's Spirit is not present.

A minister friend told me about a startling awakening he had while reading the ordination-renewal form his denomination had sent him. As he scanned the questions on the application, it dawned on him there was no measurement for spiritual things. Instead, the questions consisted of, "How many people attend your services on Sundays? How much growth has your church experienced? What percentage of that growth is reflected in your budget? What is the amount given per capita? What was your missions giving last year? How many are enrolled in your boys' program? How many are involved in your women's auxiliary? How many times did you preach in the past year?"

Not a word was mentioned about the pastor's prayer life or the church's, for that matter. Not a single question was raised about where the pastor might be in his walk with God. Nothing was asked about the spiritual condition of the minister's family or congregation, about his morals and relationships in the church, about his spiritual burdens and the spiritual growth of his sheep.

My friend could have been a reprobate or an adulterer and still passed his denomination's test, simply by filling out the application.

Needless to say, I was shocked and amazed to see how far removed this denomination's leaders were from any understanding of what the true church of Jesus Christ is about. I believe certain features distinguish our Lord's true church, and I want to give you several examples from scripture.

The basic pattern of Christ's true church is found in the gospel of John. The true church of Jesus Christ is comprised of believers who have a special love relationship with their Lord.

"Mary Magdalene came and told the disciples that she had seen the Lord, and that he had spoken these things unto her. Then the same day at evening, being the first day of the week, when the doors were shut where the disciples were assembled for fear of the Jews, came Jesus and stood in the midst, and saith unto them, Peace be unto you. And when he had so said, he shewed unto them his hands and his side. Then were the disciples glad, when they saw the Lord.

"Then said Jesus to them again, Peace be unto you: as my Father hath sent me, even so send I you. And when he had said this, he breathed on them, and saith unto them, Receive ye the Holy Ghost: Whose soever sins ye remit, they are remitted unto them; and whose soever sins ye retain, they are retained" (John 20:18-23).

This passage describes the first gathering of the saints after Jesus' resurrection. It was literally the first meeting of Christ's church. In this gathering, we can see all the basic features that have comprised the Lord's church throughout history.

All of those believers in that first meeting had focused their lives solely on Jesus. They had given up all the love of the world to be with him. He was more important to them even than their own families. They based their very lives on every word he spoke. Everyone there could truly say, "For me, to live is Christ."

Luke's account of the gathering implies that more were present than just the eleven disciples. This gathering also possibly included Joseph of Arimathea, Nicodemus, some of the seventy appointed disciples, some from the town of Bethany including Mary and Lazarus and their family, and even Jesus' own brothers. The common threads that identified these faithful followers were a consuming devotion to the man Jesus Christ, a fresh vision of their Lord in resurrection power and a heart that burned for his word.

Simon Peter was there, and we know he had incredible revelations of Jesus. He had spent three years with Christ daily, and he'd seen him transfigured with Moses and Elijah on the mount. We also know that Mary Magdalene had personal revelations of Jesus, both before and after his resurrection. He had cast seven demons out of her, and later he revealed himself to her outside the tomb. The two disciples who returned from Emmaus might have been at this gathering also. They too had received a glorious revelation of Christ as they walked along the road. They testified to the disciples that Jesus had expounded to them all the things scripture said about him (see Luke 24:27), and afterward his word burned in their hearts.

Whoever was in that room — the converted harlot, the physician Luke, the fishermen who dropped their nets to follow Jesus, the publican Nicodemus, the wealthy Joseph, poor widows, or a resurrected Lazarus — everyone present had a special love relationship with the Lord.

Peter and the other disciples may have served as leaders of the group, but they alone didn't have a revelation of Christ that they passed along to the others. No, everyone there had had a special, personal encounter with him. What a wonderful scene this gathering provided. Here in the midst of great apostasy, gross darkness, hatred for the son of God and rejection of his love, the Lord had a people completely devoted to him.

So it is today. All over the world in every nation and ethnic group, in every walk of life, among rich and poor and people of all races, the Lord has individuals who are wholly devoted to him just as he did in that first meeting. In a time of chaos and spiritual darkness, his people are drawing closer, becoming more intimate with him.

Whenever I travel to other nations, I invariably meet other Christians. Some immediately hug me or grab my hand and cry, "Praise the Lord, I'm a Christian too! It's so good to meet another brother in Christ."

In some cases, however, it doesn't take long for me to discern we don't share a true spiritual bond. As our conversation deepens, they speak only of their good life, their recent promotion, their exciting vacation. They never offer even a single sign of having a devoted heart for Jesus. It becomes apparent they are not a part of that vast, invisible body of sold-out, wholly devoted lovers of Christ.

At times I've entered foreign prayer meetings where the people were praising the Lord boldly, and I thought, "I've found the Lord's church!" As soon as the pastor got up to speak, though, I realized he wasn't devoted to Christ. Everything he said was of the flesh. Therefore, the bond of God's Spirit simply wasn't present. It was not really "his" church.

I've often wondered what would happen if Jesus came in the flesh and I asked him to reveal to me his true church. I believe he would take me on a tour from church to church, showing me congregations large and small. Yet of these many churches, he would point to only a few along the way and say, "That is my church."

I have no doubt I would be utterly shocked. I might ask, "Lord, what of those other thousands who are singing love songs to you?"

He would answer, "They are not devoted to me. They

have a form of worship but no genuine heart-love. They're all words and no deeds, with no real thirst for my truth. No, that is not my church."

Can Jesus point to you and say to the host of heaven, "Look at him. There is my church, my habitation. Behold how he yearns after me. I've been speaking to him for years, and he still yearns for more. Look at his hunger. Look at how my word is his delight! See how he has proven his love by his obedience to my word.

"Now behold my other servant. Look at how she waits alone in her prayer room. She's yearning for a fresh touch from me. I not only have first place in her life, but I am everything to her. I'm the center of her focus, her very life." In God's true church, the Holy Spirit is at work producing a spirit of forgiveness and love in the body of Christ.

Scripture says that after the resurrection, Jesus breathed on his disciples and said, "...Receive ye the Holy Ghost" (John 20:22). In essence, Christ was saying, "The Holy Spirit is my very breath."

We know that at this time Jesus was building his church by using these very people as his living stones. He was laying the foundation upon which all works of the gospel would be done in the future. The very special work of the Spirit in this passage undoubtedly has great significance.

We can gather from the context that Jesus' act was meant to prepare his followers as his testimony to a lost world. Notice the verse that immediately follows his breathing of God's Spirit on them: "Whose soever sins ye remit, they are remitted unto them; and whose soever sins ye retain, they are retained" (John 20:23).

We know only the Lord can forgive sins so what could Jesus possibly mean by this? The "remitting of sins"

Christ refers to here are those sins committed against us by others. He wants his mercy and forgiveness to be manifest in us so that the whole world will witness in us his love and readiness to forgive. By this we show Christ's mercy to sinful people.

Once again, Jesus set the example for us, this time at the cross. In that horrible, agonizing moment, he prayed, "Father, forgive them; for they know not what they do" (Luke 23:34). In this single sentence, Christ absolved his murderers completely, saying, "Father, no matter what other sins these men have to answer to you for, I release them from guilt on this matter." Now when judgment day comes, not one of those soldiers, priests or leaders will have to answer for Jesus' crucifixion, all because he said, "I remit this sin!"

This was the spirit of Stephen as he was being stoned. Scripture says, "He kneeled down, and cried with a loud voice, Lord, lay not this sin to their charge" (Acts 7:60). Stephen too was saying, "Father, please wipe this sin of theirs off your books. I remit it in heaven."

Why does Jesus say we are to do this? Simply put, he's explaining to us, "I'm building my church on a foundation of forgiving mercy. Your readiness to forgive those who sin against you is your witness for me.

"As you go forth devoted to me – doing my will, bearing fruit, being useful to my body – you are going to be persecuted, misunderstood, mocked, beaten, killed. You'll be called the offscouring of the world. Your flesh will want to retaliate. You'll want to fight back, to defend yourself. Even your brothers and sisters in the faith, the religious ones, will mistreat you. They'll cheat you, speak against you, wound you, crush your spirit. You'll think you have a right to defend yourself, and you'll want to act in your flesh and strike back.

"But I am demanding something of my church that is impossible to do without the very breath and anointing of my Spirit. You simply can't do this in your own strength. I am commanding you to remit every sin that a brother or sister or even a sinner commits against you. I'll have mercy on those to whom you show mercy. All who sin against the Father and against grace will answer to him for their trespasses; but whatever sin you remit that has been committed against you, I will forgive!"

The church of Jesus Christ is a house where there is no place for vengeance. It's a place where every devoted child of God has released from his heart his enemies' sins and has asked God to release them as well. He has no hurts or grudges remaining. That is the powerful witness of Christ's body to his glory. "We forgive those who sin against us, even as we have been forgiven!"

We talk about revival, and we pray for a greater out-pouring of God's Holy Spirit on the church. But too often we settle for the spectacular, the visible, the outward manifestations. A true revival is an awesome manifestation of the presence of Jesus in which we are convicted of our bitterness, grudges, prayerlessness and deadness to the word of God. There is no work worthy of the word "revival" or "awakening" without this purifying manifestation of forgiveness and total devotion to Christ.

You can see how important it is for all of God's people to have the presence of Christ manifested in them at all times. His Spirit alone can give us the power to forgive all grudges, to offer grace, mercy, forgiveness and restoration to all who have wronged us. Therefore, we must be engulfed in God's spirit of grace at all times!

In this wilderness of economic hardship and scarcity,

God is going to renew his vows of love and marriage with his bride.

"I will betroth thee unto me for ever; yea, I will betroth thee unto me in righteousness, and in judgment, and in lovingkindness, and in mercies. I will even betroth thee unto me in faithfulness: and thou shalt know the Lord" (Hosea 2:19-20).

The Lord is telling the church, "There was a time when you loved me with all your heart. You treated me the way a bridegroom should be treated. You had no other lovers, and you were faithful to me. But now you've taken on other loves, and I'm going to remove them all from you. I'm going to isolate you so there's no one left but you and me. I'm going to get back the devotion from you that I've longed for. You're going to get to know me again."

Try to imagine a time when God's people will not be able to afford monthly internet charges, or movies, or videos...when every dollar has to be spent on bare essentials...when people spend hours on their knees, praying for their daily supplies because they have no other means. When that time comes, there won't be any money available for frivolous pursuits. Suddenly, being in God's house will be the highlight of life. We'll be drawn close to our father through prayer, and we'll be awed by the miraculous help he sends us.

God reminded Israel they loved him most when they were in the wilderness of deprivation. "...Thus saith the Lord; I remember thee, the kindness of thy youth, the love of thine espousals, when thou wentest after me in the wilderness, in a land that was not sown" (Jeremiah 2:2). He was telling them, "You were in a barren wilderness, a dead, lifeless place. There was no wheat, barley or beans, not even any grass, and yet it was in this barren place that you first became my love. I became the center of your life, and you pursued me with all your heart. You loved me tenderly because I was everything to you. Don't you remember, Israel? You learned to love me in a place of total scarcity." "Israel was holiness unto the Lord..." (Jeremiah 2:3).

God reminded Israel of how they turned to sin after he had showered them with blessings. "I brought you into a plentiful country, to eat the fruit thereof and the goodness thereof; but when ye entered, ye defiled my land, and made mine heritage an abomination" (Jeremiah 2:7). Once Israel experienced great prosperity, "...the pastors...transgressed against me, and the prophets...walked after things that do not profit" (Jeremiah 2:8). God was saying, in essence, "You were so different when I took you into the wilderness. You treated me as a loving bride should treat her bridegroom. But prosperity and blessings spoiled you. They stole your heart from me."

This is exactly what has happened to our generation of the church in America. Prosperity has robbed us of our passionate love for Jesus. We've taken God's blessings for granted, and now everyone is out for himself. The nominal church, including entire denominations, has become lazy, lukewarm, corrupt, blasphemous, believing it has no need of God.

What did God do to Israel in this situation? He told them, "Wherefore I will yet plead with you, saith the Lord, and with your children's children will I plead" (Jeremiah 2:9). He was telling them, "I'm taking you back to the wilderness. When we get there, I'm going to plead with you once again to return to me, to be mine, to be faithful."

This prophecy includes us today. A worldwide depression could easily be God's way of leading his church back into a wilderness. Once he gets us there, he will plead with us to return to our first love. He wants us to rest in him, to put our total trust in him, to love him as our faithful, protective, providing bridegroom. Here is what Isaiah says God will do for us in that wilderness.

"Strengthen ye the weak hands, and confirm the feeble knees. Say to them that are of a fearful heart, Be strong, fear not: behold, your God will come with vengeance, even God with a recompense; he will come and save you. Then the eyes of the blind shall be opened, and the ears of the deaf shall be unstopped. Then shall the lame man leap as a hart, and the tongue of the dumb sing: for in the wilderness shall waters break out, and streams in the desert.

"And the parched ground shall become a pool, and the thirsty land springs of water: in the habitation of dragons, where each lay, shall be grass with reeds and rushes. And a highway shall be there, and a way, and it shall be called the way of holiness; the unclean shall not pass over it; but it shall be for those: the wayfaring men, though fools, shall not err therein.

"No lion shall be there, nor any ravenous beast shall go up thereon, it shall not be found there; but the redeemed shall walk there: and the ransomed of the Lord shall return, and come to Zion with songs and everlasting joy upon their heads: they shall obtain joy and gladness, and sorrow and sighing shall flee away" (Isaiah 35:3-10).

Yes, our God is going to do all of this for us in our wilderness. May his blessed word drive out any fear in your heart so that you return to him in faith and love.

CHAPTER TWELVE

FINDING REST
AMID DIFFICULTIES

The ministry of a watchman is to see what is coming and to alert the people by blowing the trumpet call of warning from the city walls. It is also the calling of a watchman to supply the people with every bit of information he has. At times he may become too excited or emotional by what he sees – for instance, he may see a powerful tornado gathering on the horizon – and blow the trumpet too loudly, piercing the people's ears. Still he must warn. Once he has alerted the people, his work is done. Regardless of whether the people ignore or heed his warning, he is obligated to inform, warn and alert them.

All of the Old Testament prophets were watchmen. The Spirit of God fell upon them and showed them the awesome judgments coming upon their nation: pestilences, famines, judgments, wars, shakings. In their mind's eye, these watchmen would see invading armies sweeping down on Israel. To accurately warn the people, they would describe the very sound of the enemy horses' hoof beats. Even today when we read their prophetic writings, we can almost hear the sounds of war. Their prophecies were meant to be full of emotional impact in order to stir the people to heed God's warning.

Today we picture the prophets of old as having long faces and bulging veins, shouting their warnings like angry madmen.

Yet I believe we have totally misjudged these prophets, especially Jeremiah and Ezekiel. As I have studied the lives of the Old Testament prophets, I've found them all to be among the most balanced, well-adjusted people in the Bible. Judgment was not their only message. They got just as emotional and excited when they spoke about the love and mercy of God toward his people.

The prophets never allowed their messages of judgment to dominate their thoughts or preached to the point that it was all they ever spoke about. The prophets were just as informed about the great mercies and lovingkindness of God as they were about his fierce anger and wrath. Yes, we read passages that describe these men trembling, quaking, their "bowels boiling"; but God's prophets were also extremely joyful in the Lord. In fact, they were more anxious to alert the people of God to his mercies than to his judgments.

Consider Isaiah. In chapter 24, the prophet moans, "Woe is me! I see so much treachery all around, and now everything is being shaken to its very foundation. The Lord is turning it all upside down, spoiling everything in sight. All joy is darkened, all mirth is gone. The earth is reeling to and fro like a drunken man. God is punishing the earth."

In this chapter, Isaiah does the work of a watchman: he's on the wall, and he describes what he sees coming, something that hasn't happened yet. He's grieved and deeply pained by what he sees. He says it leaves him "lean," meaning "emaciated." It's so terrifying, it hurts

Secure

him even to declare the news; but now, having delivered his soul, he is free from all blood-guiltiness. Notice how quickly he moves to address God's mercy.

"O Lord, thou art my God; I will exalt thee, I will praise thy name; for thou hast done wonderful things; thy counsels of old are faithfulness and truth...Thou hast been a strength to the poor, a strength to the needy in his distress, a refuge from the storm, a shadow from the heat, when the blast of the terrible ones is as a storm against the wall...

"He will swallow up death in victory; and the Lord God will wipe away tears from off all faces; and the rebuke of his people shall he take away from off all the earth: for the Lord hath spoken it.

"And it shall be said in that day, Lo, this is our God; we have waited for him, and he will save us: this is the Lord; we have waited for him, we will be glad and rejoice in his salvation" (Isaiah 25:1, 4, 8-9).

These aren't the words of a dour, nay-saying sourpuss. They obviously come from the heart of a joyful man. Isaiah could say, "I've done my part. I've warned you about what's coming, but I also want you to know what a wonderfully merciful God we serve."

Now let's consider Jeremiah. He's called the "gloom and doom" prophet because he spoke the most terrifying warnings in all of scripture. He was the man called upon to pronounce the fall of Jerusalem, the destruction of the temple and the seventy years of captivity. He warned the people by using horribly violent images. He prophesied, "I see armies coming, thundering through the city, tearing down the walls, leveling everything to the ground. You're all going to be left so destitute, you'll end up boiling and eating your own babies!"

The Lord instructed Jeremiah to speak this harsh message to Israel in a time of great prosperity. Everything was going fine for them. Why should they believe such things could happen? When Jeremiah prophesied these things, the people mocked him, laughing and jeering. Nobody wanted to hear the message. After a while, the prophet himself grew weary of preaching it.

God's fiery wrath and judgment, however, were not Jeremiah's only message. This man was also a powerful preacher of God's love and mercy.

He said, "I will restore health unto thee, and I will heal thee of thy wounds, saith the Lord; because they called thee an outcast, saying, This is Zion, whom no man seeketh after. Thus saith the Lord; Behold, I will bring again the captivity of Jacob's tents, and have mercy on his dwelling places; and the city shall be builded upon her own heap, and the palace shall remain after the manner thereof.

"And out of them shall proceed thanksgiving and the voice of them that make merry: and I will multiply them, and they shall not be few; I will also glorify them, and they shall not be small. Their children also shall be as aforetime, and their congregation shall be established before me, and I will punish all that oppress them.

"And their nobles shall be of themselves, and their governor shall proceed from the midst of them; and I will cause him to draw near, and he shall approach unto me: for who is this that engaged his heart to approach unto me? saith the Lord. And ye shall be my people, and I will be your God" (Jeremiah 30:17-22).

Jeremiah was always talking about restoration, health, cures, rebuilding. These aspects of his prophesies revealed God's heart toward his people. The Lord told his people through this man, "Like as I have brought all this great evil upon this people, so will I bring upon them all the good that I have promised them" (Jeremiah 32:42). Jeremiah wasn't just a preacher of judgment. He was also a preacher of mercy. He said, "Just as surely as I tell you that judgment is coming, I'm also going to tell you repentance will bring forth God's goodness, grace and mercy."

These are not the words of a man who went around moaning and groaning his whole lifetime. Yes, Jeremiah cried aloud his warnings of judgment; he never compromised the vital message of God's consuming hatred for sin. Jeremiah wasn't obsessed with that message, though. No man could have spoken such powerful promises of restoration, grace and goodness without having a joyful heart, full of peace and rest.

We are to be alerted and warned by prophetic messages, and we're to heed every one that's revealed and confirmed in scripture. We're to gather all the knowledge we can about the coming storm so we can prepare our hearts for whatever destruction it brings, but we are not to let fear or anxiety consume our thinking, dominate our minds, take hold of our hearts. We are to listen carefully to the warnings of the watchmen but are not to become obsessed with their warnings.

Darkness is certainly coming, and judgment is at our very door. As God's people, we cannot allow any cloud of darkness to hide the light of his great promises of love and mercy toward his people. We are to be well informed by the Lord's word and prophets, but we are not to dwell on prophetic knowledge so much that it takes over our lives. The devil would love for that to happen. He knows if he can't get you to doubt God's word concerning his judgment, he'll take you to another extreme by driving you to a fearful obsession with perilous times. He'll try to rob you of all hope by consuming you with thoughts of foreboding. He'll convince you that you can figure out the future through the study of prophecy, but in reality he wants you addicted to fear. He wants you obsessed with subjects such as Armageddon, the Antichrist and the mark of the beast so you're constantly worried, thinking, "Will I have to take the mark to survive? Or will I be able to buy or sell without it?"

The apostle Paul reassures us about such things with this instruction. "Finally, brethren, whatsoever things are true, whatsoever things are honest, whatsoever things are just, whatsoever things are pure, whatsoever things are lovely, whatsoever things are of good report; if there be any virtue, and if there be any praise, think on these things" (Philippians 4:8). Paul is telling us, "You've heard all the warnings. Now, simply take heed to what God's word reveals and to what his watchmen are saying. Finally, fix all your thoughts on Jesus and his goodness."

I have warned that Christians are going to suffer, that there will be great loss and hardship; and right now multitudes of precious saints all over the world are enduring unbelievable tribulation.

But none of these things is the focus of all my energies and ministry. No, the deepest expression of my soul is to proclaim the love of God the father and the tender mercy of our savior Jesus.

I know the stock market is going to collapse eventually. I know the American lifestyle and the lifestyles of all prosperous nations will have to change one day. I know everything is going to reel and shake, but I don't get up in the morning worrying, "What are we going to eat? What are we going to wear? What about heat, light, security?"

Jesus warned us not to do that. When I go to bed at night, I sleep like a baby. I know I'm not God and that he alone is in control of all these things. I simply do what the prophet Isaiah did; he put his mind to rest by fully trusting in his Lord. He said, "Thou wilt keep him in perfect peace, whose mind is stayed on thee: because he trusteth in thee" (Isaiah 26:3).

I have never considered myself a prophet, and I wouldn't be worthy even to be a servant to the holy Isaiah, but I know something of how this man must have felt. He had reason to become downcast and hopeless because the people he preached to didn't respond to God's warnings of judgment. Even when God removed their prosperity and everything began to reel and shake, they still weren't moved. Instead, their hearts became only more hardened.

As Isaiah saw God once again prospering and favoring Israel in spite of his warnings of judgment, he recognized it as a final wake-up call to the slumbering nation. Isaiah saw a people who once were righteous but now were wicked, rejecting God's mercy, blessing and care. The prophet said, "Let favour be shewed to the wicked, yet will he not learn righteousness; in the land of uprightness will he deal unjustly, and will not behold the majesty of the Lord" (Isaiah 26:10).

As Isaiah surveyed the drastic situation, he concluded, "How will God get through to his people? They won't respond to the famines and pestilences. They refuse to acknowledge the Lord's hand in it all. They think it's just happenstance. When God prospers them, they think, 'Look at what my own hands have accomplished!'"

We see this attitude throughout the world today. We have witnessed nations battered by storms, tidal waves, hurricanes, earthquakes, famines, pestilences, all kinds of methods God has used to try to get people's attention. Yet there still has not been a move toward the Lord in response. Here in America, we've witnessed years of incredible prosperity as God calls us one last time to learn righteousness and return to him, but it seems to have been to no avail.

Still, Isaiah never gave up hope for Israel. He said in the midst of the judgment, "…the Lord of hosts shall reign in mount Zion, and in Jerusalem…gloriously" (Isaiah 24:23). He was shouting with joy, "God is still in control!"

The Lord is still in control today. It shouldn't matter to us what awful news we see or hear in the media. We have to know in our hearts that God is reigning gloriously in Zion. He's on the throne, sitting as king over the flood.

Isaiah knew that when favor and prosperity failed to awaken the people to righteousness, God would send severe judgments. These judgments would so far surpass anything they'd seen, everyone would know God was behind it: "…for when thy judgments are in the earth, the inhabitants of the world will learn righteousness" (Isaiah 26:9).

I read an incredible quote by a Hollywood producer who has a reputation for partying beyond all limits with drugs, alcohol and sex. This man said, "Things have become so debauched today, divine retribution has to intervene." This man stays drunk all the time, and yet God is using him to speak to the world. Even the heathen are crying, "Things have become so wild now, judgment has to fall from heaven."

What are the righteous to do when all of these things come down on wicked humankind? In a time when great judgments were falling on the nation all around him,

Isaiah testified he had a double portion of peace. A similarly wonderful outlook is available to all today who trust in God and put their minds at rest in the Lord.

In the twelve preceding chapters, Isaiah prophesies to a number of nations, including Judah and Jerusalem, telling of horrible judgments to come. In one of these prophecies, Isaiah warns of the collapse of the world's greatest power, Babylon. At the time, such a thing seemed impossible. Babylon seemed too rich, too powerful, too prosperous to fall. Everyone wondered, "How could this superpower fall into ruin and be brought to the ground as Isaiah says?"

Isaiah prophesied about a chain reaction of events among the nations. First, Moab was to be judged, then Tyre and Damascus. Afterward, Egypt was to fall, followed by Arabia and Tarshish. Next, Israel, Judah and Jerusalem would be judged. Finally, Babylon would fall. God was going to shake the whole earth, just as he said he would; and before it was all over, people in every nation would be mourning.

In his mind's eye, Isaiah had foreseen all of this coming. You might think that someone who foresaw this kind of future would be so devastated, he couldn't even continue his ministry. Surely Isaiah was overwhelmed by what he saw. But, scripture reveals, at this very time the prophet enjoyed great peace. How did he come into such a place of peace?

As the judgments were poised to strike the nations, Isaiah was shut in with God in prayer. "Yea, in the way of thy judgments, O Lord, have we waited for thee; the desire of our soul is to thy name, and to the remembrance of thee" (Isaiah 26:8). Isaiah was prepared for anything because he was on his knees, waiting on the Lord.

What are you waiting for?

Are you waiting to see whether you survive the storm or not? Are you waiting nervously, fearing you might lose your job, your home, your savings? Or, are you waiting on the Lord, as Isaiah did? If you're waiting on our heavenly father, then you're gaining strength because your mind is stayed on him. He's revealing his power to you in the secret closet of prayer. He is encouraging you that you will make it through.

The truth is there's no way on earth any of us can work ourselves into a place of trust. Willpower alone cannot produce faith in God.

Rather, faith and trust are the fruit of an intimate seeking of the Lord. It is a gift bestowed on those who hunger after Jesus, who crave his continual presence in their lives.

In the opinion of one Puritan writer, seeking the Lord in prayer isn't optional for believers. He wrote, "The person is not saved who neglects prayer. He is an atheist." In other words, "I don't care how much a man or woman claims to know Christ. If he or she neglects the prayer closet, that person is not even a Christian."

Isaiah was a man of prayer. Because he spent time in the Lord's presence, he could say with confidence, "I see frightful judgments and terrible shakings falling on the nations. I tremble at the sight of so much suffering, with multitudes overwhelmed by fear. Yet there are even more judgments to come, which are almost unspeakable.

"However, none of these things dominates my thinking. None of them can remove me from the perfect peace I have in the Lord. In the midst of all this turmoil, I've been waiting on him, drawing nigh to him. The more time I spend with him, the more I look back and remember all of his faithfulness and miracles of the past. That's why

I'm not consumed by thoughts of all these terrible judgments. My mind is totally consumed by my God."

It is not God's will that any of his children face the perilous times ahead with fear and trembling. The Lord does not desire these prophecies and warnings to scare or frighten us. Rather, here is Jesus' heart on the matter, stated very plainly, "Peace I leave with you, my peace I give unto you: not as the world giveth, give I unto you. Let not your heart be troubled, neither let it be afraid" (John 14:27).

In Matthew, Jesus himself prophesied of coming events in the world, events that sounded most frightful. He spoke of wars, pestilence and earthquakes in various places. He warned his hearers, "You'll be afflicted, some of you even killed. Iniquity will abound. False prophets and messiahs shall arise, deceiving many." (Even today there are many "pillow prophets" in the land, men who preach, "It's the year of jubilee, and God wants to pay all of your debts. Let's party! Don't worry about anything because by year's end, you'll be totally debt-free." I wonder what their poor followers will do at the end of the year, when their debts are piled higher than ever. Jubilee isn't about that kind of redemption of debts. It's about Christ's redeeming power to set us free from the debt of sin, not from the debt of Sears or J.C. Penney's.)

Later in Matthew, Jesus explains his reasons for forewarning us about all of these catastrophic events. He says, "I'm telling you all these things so you'll believe in me when you see them come to pass." He wasn't trying to put a burden of fear on us or to motivate us to holiness by frightening us. He simply doesn't want us to be surprised when we're hit by awful storms. He doesn't want our faith to be shipwrecked when we suddenly face incredible suffering. Most of all, he wants us to believe there is a Lord over all these awful things, a God who's loving enough to warn us about them and keep us through them all.

When Isaiah alerted the people that judgment was coming, he wasn't waiting around for the hard times to appear. He was looking beyond them all, to a greater vision God had given him. Isaiah saw his Lord coming to wipe away the tears of his children, remove their burdens and deliver them from all guilt, fear and reproach.

"And it shall be said in that day, Lo, this is our God; we have waited for him, and he will save us: this is the Lord; we have waited for him, we will be glad and rejoice in his salvation... He will swallow up death in victory; and the Lord God will wipe away tears from off all faces; and the rebuke of his people shall he take away from off all the earth: for the Lord hath spoken it" (Isaiah 25:9, 8).

Isaiah also had a prophetic message for believers of all ages. Isaiah was saying to us in this passage, "You who live in the very last days can also have this double portion of peace. Simply trust in Christ Jesus, your rock."

"Trust ye in the Lord for ever: for in the Lord Jehovah is everlasting strength" (Isaiah 26:4). The Hebrew meaning of this phrase is, "Trust in Jehovah, who is the rock of ages." "Behold, God is my salvation; I will trust, and not be afraid: for the Lord Jehovah is my strength and my song; he also is become my salvation" (Isaiah 12:2).

I've searched and studied the scriptures; I've pleaded with the Lord to give me a message of hope and encouragement for his people. At one point, I pored over the Psalms, marking every promise of divine protection and preservation I could find. I searched out other promises in the prophets, in Deuteronomy, in Nehemiah, wherever I might find a word of reassurance to God's people.

All of the promises I found were indeed comforting and faith-building, yet my spirit still cried out, "Oh, Lord, please speak a word to my heart for your children. You alone have the words of eternal life, just as Peter said. Only you can speak a word of comfort to us right now."

One day, the Holy Spirit answered my prayer. He spoke the following words to my heart: "I'm going to give you a single promise from my word. And if you will commit your very life to it, this word will keep you through any and all perilous times."

I know if we will embrace this one verse, fully believing it, it will be our daily power-source of faith. Here is the promise the Spirit showed me: "...your Father knoweth what things ye have need of, before ye ask him" (Matthew 6:8).

In Luke 12, Jesus enumerates the things he says our heavenly father knows we need. Those needs are, in short, food, drink and clothing. "...Therefore I say unto you, Take no thought for your life, what ye shall eat; neither for the body, what ye shall put on...If then God so clothe the grass, which is today in the field, and tomorrow is cast into the oven; how much more will he clothe you, O ye of little faith?" (Luke 12:22, 28).

The word for "clothe" here means "shelter." Jesus is saying, "Take a look at the grass in your yard. It's full and green today, but tomorrow you'll mow it and collect it. Well, I bring the greenness to that grass. I give it life and care for it as long as it's there. Don't you think I care for your needs better than I do for this grass? Don't you realize I know full well what you need, whether it's food or clothes? Don't you see you matter much more to me than anything in this world?"

Jesus added, "All these things do the nations of the

world seek after: and your Father knoweth that ye have need of these things" (Luke 12:30). Again, Christ reminds us, "Here is all you need to know: Your heavenly father knows what your needs are. He has already enumerated them."

When Jesus says, "Take no thought for your life, what you shall eat...," he isn't suggesting we forego all preparation for the future. The Greek meaning of this phrase is, "Let it not distract you. Don't be overanxious about it. Don't let it become your focus." These needs are not to preoccupy us. Jesus promises, "Rather seek ye the kingdom of God; and all these things shall be added unto you. Fear not, little flock..." (Luke 12:31-32). The Greek word for "added" here means to "proceed further than promised." If we will simply trust him, our Lord will bless us with more than we need.

When Israel was in the wilderness, they murmured against the Lord, saying, "You've brought our children out here to die." God answered them, "No. Instead, you're going to die in the wilderness because of your unbelief, but I will save your children."

If you're concerned for your family's welfare in the coming days, I've got good news for you; your children are God's children, and he cares more for your loved ones than you do. He knows exactly what you all need to survive. He knows about your need to have a roof over your head, and he knows exactly what your rent bill or mortgage payment is each month. He knows about the mouths you have to feed, and he knows the amount of food you need in your cupboard. You can trust him fully to meet all of these needs because he promises to. Paul writes, "My God shall supply all your need according to his riches in glory by Christ Jesus" (Philippians 4:19). The word "supply" here, as used in the Greek, means "to cram, to over-meet." This is in keeping with God's promise to us in Ephesians. "Now unto him that is able to do exceeding abundantly above all that we ask or think, according to the power that worketh in us" (Ephesians 3:20).

Tragically, many people will grow bitter because God won't answer their prayers to protect their wealth. Such people have never known suffering, and they'll think God has failed them. But the Lord says to rich and poor alike, "Seek me first! Forget about all your worldly possessions. Get alone with me, search my word, seek my face. Then go to my house and enjoy the wonderful, fulfilling fellowship I've provided for you there. I'm going to take care of all the things you're worried about. You will be supplied the essentials to get by."

There is one lesson every believer must learn and practice. At any given moment, world events are moving so fast nobody can really keep up with them. In truth, nobody knows what's going to happening in the future, and I'll be perfectly honest, when I think about these frightening things coming, my flesh gets scared. I don't want to see disasters taking place.

Yet here is our final lesson, and my faith is anchored in this: My heavenly father knows me. He knows exactly what I need and when I need it, and the very fact he knows this is proof enough I am forever under his care. Daniel said of the Lord, "...he knoweth what is in the darkness, and the light dwelleth with him" (Daniel 2:22).

God knows all about the dark days ahead. He knows the darkness can't hide his face from us. Indeed, our path through hard times will be found only in him, and he's calling us today to have a childlike trust in his faithfulness. He will supply every need for his beloved children!

CHAPTER THIRTEEN

FINAL THOUGHTS

At a ministers conference, a pastor approached me with a troubled look on his face. He said, "I read your book, *America's Last Call*, and I'm concerned. If what you say is true about a depression looming ahead, then what am I supposed to do about my new church-building program? We've just started construction on a multimillion-dollar structure. If the economy is doomed to fall into a depression, as you say, where does that leave our project? Are you suggesting we just shut everything down and quit?"

I hear similar questions from businesspeople, investors and young entrepreneurs. "Fear is mounting all around, and businesses are cutting back. So, what should we do? Should we shut everything down and retreat into a survival mode? If we act in fear, merely holding on, what's left?"

Here is my answer to these kinds of questions: If the Lord tells you to move ahead with a project, do it! If he tells you to launch a building program or make an investment or expand, do it. Whatever God's Spirit directs, God himself will provide for.

Jesus instructed us, "...Occupy till I come" (Luke 19:13). The Greek word for "occupy" here means "trade, stay busy." Our Lord's word clearly instructs us to work while it is yet day, to provide for our households and not to fear the unknown. While we are doing this, we are to seek him with all our heart, mind and strength, to pray in faith, asking for direction, and to believe the Holy Spirit will speak a word to our inner man, saying, "This is the way. Walk in it!"

The evangelist Aimee Simple McPherson built Angeles Temple during the midst of the Great Depression in the 1930s. Numerous other churches were built during that same period as well, and new businesses were started by young entrepreneurs then. The Holy Spirit helped his praying people in many creative ways during that time. Today, we who call ourselves by our savior's name dare not be paralyzed by fear in any form. We're to seek his direction, obtain his mind and move forward in faith.

In this book, I've written that as Christians we must put our trust wholly in the Lord as we face hard times. Already in nations that are deep in depression, believers are seeing God prove himself as Jehovah-Jireh, their great provider. The Lord is providing sufficient means and working incredible miracles for those who trust him in the midst of all chaos.

I've also written that I believe Christians in America ought to prepare wisely for the future. This means we may need to store food, if we're so led by God's Spirit and if our confidence doesn't rest in our provisions. No one can accurately predict how our country may be impacted by economic hardships, epidemics and environmental calamities. I personally believe these current disruptions may not be as disastrous as some predict; but in the years ahead, conditions could become chaotic as problems begin to mount on a worldwide scale. This could lead to a meltdown so severe that there may come a cry for a world leader, a kind of czar, to restore financial stability. If this kind of scenario comes to pass, the world's major cities would be hit the hardest. If U.S. government fails, many social services could be delayed or even cut off and riots could break out.

If we panic about our personal finances or investments, we'll grieve our heavenly father deeply. Our fretting betrays a fearful attitude that says we don't truly believe he can take care of us. Now it is more important than ever for us to entrust our futures and families into his loving hands.

God help us all to rest in his glorious promises!

Scriptures to Live by in Perilous Times

PSALM 9:8-10

He shall judge the world in righteousness, he shall minister judgment to the people in uprightness. The Lord also will be a refuge for the oppressed, a refuge in times of trouble. And they that know thy name will put their trust in thee: for thou, Lord, hast not forsaken them that seek thee.

PSALM 12:5-7

For the oppression of the poor, for the sighing of the needy, now will I arise, saith the Lord; I will set him in safety from him that puffeth at him. The words of the Lord are pure words: as silver tried in a furnace of earth, purified seven times. Thou shalt keep them, O Lord, thou shalt preserve them from this generation for ever.

PSALM 18:19

He brought me forth also into a large place; he delivered me, because he delighted in me.

PSALM 16:7-9

I will bless the Lord, who hath given me counsel: my reins also instruct me in the night seasons. I have set the

Lord always before me: because he is at my right hand, I shall not be moved. Therefore my heart is glad, and my glory rejoiceth: my flesh also shall rest in hope.

PSALM 17:7-8

Shew thy marvellous lovingkindness, O thou that savest by thy right hand them which put their trust in thee from those that rise up against them. Keep me as the apple of the eye, hide me under the shadow of thy wings.

PSALM 20:6-9

Now know I that the Lord saveth his anointed; he will hear him from his holy heaven with the saving strength of his right hand. Some trust in chariots, and some in horses: but we will remember the name of the Lord our God. They are brought down and fallen: but we are risen, and stand upright. Save, Lord: let the king hear us when we call.

PSALM 22:4-5

Our fathers trusted in thee: they trusted, and thou didst deliver them. They cried unto thee, and were delivered: they trusted in thee, and were not confounded.

PSALM 27:5

In the time of trouble he shall hide me in his pavilion: in the secret of his tabernacle shall he hide me; he shall set me up upon a rock.

PSALM 28:7-9

The Lord is my strength and my shield; my heart trusted in him, and I am helped: therefore my heart greatly rejoiceth; and with my song will I praise him. The Lord is their strength, and he is the saving strength of his anointed. Save thy people, and bless thine inheritance: feed them also, and lift them up for ever.

PSALM 31:7

I will be glad and rejoice in thy mercy: for thou hast considered my trouble; thou hast known my soul in adversities.

PSALM 32:6-8

For this shall every one that is godly pray unto thee in a time when thou mayest be found: surely in the floods of great waters they shall not come nigh unto him. Thou art my hiding place; thou shalt preserve me from trouble; thou shalt compass me about with songs of deliverance. Selah. I will instruct thee and teach thee in the way which thou shalt go: I will guide thee with mine eye.

PSALM 34:17

The righteous cry, and the Lord heareth, and delivereth them out of all their troubles.

PSALM 34:19

Many are the afflictions of the righteous: but the Lord delivereth him out of them all.

PSALM 34:6-10

This poor man cried, and the Lord heard him, and saved him out of all his troubles. The angel of the Lord encampeth round about them that fear him, and delivereth them. O taste and see that the Lord is good: blessed is the man that trusteth in him. O fear the Lord, ye his saints: for there is no want to them that fear him. The young lions do lack, and suffer hunger: but they that seek the Lord shall not want any good thing.

PSALM 34:15
The eyes of the Lord are upon the righteous, and his ears are open unto their cry.

PSALM 34:22
The Lord redeemeth the soul of his servants: and none of them that trust in him shall be desolate.

PSALM 37:3
Trust in the Lord, and do good; so shalt thou dwell in the land, and verily thou shalt be fed.

PSALM 37:18-19
The Lord knoweth the days of the upright: and their inheritance shall be for ever. They shall not be ashamed in the evil time: and in the days of famine they shall be satisfied.

PSALM 37:25
I have been young, and now am old; yet have I not seen the righteous forsaken, nor his seed begging bread.

PSALM 37:28
The Lord loveth judgment, and forsaketh not his saints; they are preserved for ever: but the seed of the wicked shall be cut off.

PSALM 46:1-3
God is our refuge and strength, a very present help in trouble. Therefore will not we fear, though the earth be

removed, and though the mountains be carried into the midst of the sea; though the waters thereof roar and be troubled, though the mountains shake with the swelling thereof.

PSALM 50:15
Call upon me in the day of trouble: I will deliver thee, and thou shalt glorify me.

PSALM 56:3-4
What time I am afraid, I will trust in thee. In God I will praise his word, in God I have put my trust; I will not fear what flesh can do unto me.

PSALM 56:11
In God have I put my trust: I will not be afraid what man can do unto me.

PSALM 56:13
Thou hast delivered my soul from death: wilt not thou deliver my feet from falling, that I may walk before God in the light of the living?

PSALM 62:5-8
My soul, wait thou only upon God; for my expectation is from him. He only is my rock and my salvation: he is my defence; I shall not be moved. In God is my salvation and my glory: the rock of my strength, and my refuge, is in God. Trust in him at all times; ye people, pour out your heart before him: God is a refuge for us.

PSALM 66:11-12
Thou broughtest us into the net; thou laidst affliction

upon our loins. Thou hast caused men to ride over our heads; we went through fire and through water: but thou broughtest us out into a wealthy place.

PSALM 66:20
Blessed be God, which hath not turned away my prayer, nor his mercy from me.

PSALM 71:3
Be thou my strong habitation, whereunto I may continually resort: thou hast given commandment to save me; for thou art my rock and my fortress.

PSALM 72:12-13
He shall deliver the needy when he crieth; the poor also, and him that hath no helper. He shall spare the poor and needy, and shall save the souls of the needy.

PSALM 78:72
He fed them according to the integrity of his heart; and guided them by the skilfulness of his hands.

PSALM 84:9
Behold, O God our shield, and look upon the face of thine anointed.

PSALM 86:7
In the day of my trouble I will call upon thee: for thou wilt answer me.

PSALM 94:14
The Lord will not cast off his people, neither will he forsake his inheritance.

PSALM 84:11-12
The Lord God is a sun and shield: the Lord will give grace and glory: no good thing will he withhold from them that walk uprightly. O Lord of hosts, blessed is the man that trusteth in thee.

PSALM 94:22
The Lord is my defence; and my God is the rock of my refuge.

PSALM 97:10
Ye that love the Lord, hate evil: he preserveth the souls of his saints; he delivereth them out of the hand of the wicked.

PSALM 102:1-2
Hear my prayer, O Lord, and let my cry come unto thee. Hide not thy face from me in the day when I am in trouble; incline thine ear unto me: in the day when I call answer me speedily.

PSALM 102:17
He will regard the prayer of the destitute, and not despise their prayer.

PSALM 103:13
Like as a father pitieth his children, so the Lord pitieth them that fear him.

PSALM 107:5-9
Hungry and thirsty, their soul fainted in them. Then they cried unto the Lord in their trouble, and he delivered them out of their distresses. And he led them forth

by the right way, that they might go to a city of habitation. Oh that men would praise the Lord for his goodness, and for his wonderful works to the children of men! For he satisfieth the longing soul, and filleth the hungry soul with goodness.

PSALM 107:20
He sent his word, and healed them, and delivered them from their destructions.

PSALM 116:6-8
The Lord preserveth the simple: I was brought low, and he helped me. Return unto thy rest, O my soul; for the Lord hath dealt bountifully with thee. For thou hast delivered my soul from death, mine eyes from tears, and my feet from falling.

PSALM 118:6
The Lord is on my side; I will not fear: what can man do unto me?

PSALM 121:1-8
I will lift up mine eyes unto the hills, from whence cometh my help. My help cometh from the Lord, which made heaven and earth. He will not suffer thy foot to be moved: he that keepeth thee will not slumber. Behold, he that keepeth Israel shall neither slumber nor sleep. The Lord is thy keeper: the Lord is thy shade upon thy right hand. The sun shall not smite thee by day, nor the moon by night. The Lord shall preserve thee from all evil: he shall preserve thy soul. The Lord shall preserve thy going out and thy coming in from this time forth, and even for evermore.

PSALM 125:1-2

They that trust in the Lord shall be as mount Zion, which cannot be removed, but abideth for ever. As the mountains are round about Jerusalem, so the Lord is round about his people from henceforth even for ever.

PSALM 127:2

It is vain for you to rise up early, to sit up late, to eat the bread of sorrows: for so he giveth his beloved sleep.

PSALM 138:8

The Lord will perfect that which concerneth me: thy mercy, O Lord, endureth for ever: forsake not the works of thine own hands.

PSALM 139:17

How precious also are thy thoughts unto me, O God! how great is the sum of them!

PSALM 141:1

Lord, I cry unto thee: make haste unto me; give ear unto my voice, when I cry unto thee.

PSALM 141:8

Mine eyes are unto thee, O God the Lord: in thee is my trust; leave not my soul destitute.

PSALM 142:5-6

I cried unto thee, O Lord: I said, Thou art my refuge and my portion in the land of the living. Attend unto my cry; for I am brought very low: deliver me from my persecutors; for they are stronger than I.

PSALM 143:8-9

Cause me to hear thy lovingkindness in the morning; for in thee do I trust: cause me to know the way wherein I should walk; for I lift up my soul unto thee. Deliver me, O Lord, from mine enemies: I flee unto thee to hide me.

PSALM 144:1-2

Blessed be the Lord my strength, which teacheth my hands to war, and my fingers to fight: My goodness, and my fortress; my high tower, and my deliverer; my shield, and he in whom I trust; who subdueth my people under me.

PSALM 145:15-16

The eyes of all wait upon thee; and thou givest them their meat in due season. Thou openest thine hand, and satisfiest the desire of every living thing.

PSALM 145:20

The Lord preserveth all them that love him: but all the wicked will he destroy.